O!
Nyo!.
Thank you
for love, support,
encouragement
You are a gift
And I'm honored
to have you in
my life

— TAKING CARE OF —
BUSINESS
WHILE MY HUSBAND IS AT THE GATE

Be BOLD!
Take care of business!
Always got your back
Es

Erick

TAKING CARE OF

BUSINESS

WHILE MY HUSBAND IS AT THE GATE

Be BOLD

Take care of business

Erickajoy
Joy

ERICKAJOY DANIELS

T.A.L.K. Publishing
5215 North Ironwood Road, Suite 200
Glendale, WI 53217
talkconsulting.net

Title: Taking Care of Business While My Husband Is At The Gate
ISBN: 978-1-7341169-9-1

Contents

Foreword

~~~~~

I absolutely love the wisdom of Solomon and his practical knowledge that he gives in the book of Proverbs. This book has given me a roadmap of insight that leads me in making wise choices in daily interactions. While it seems intuitive, I have come to realize "Every husband needs a wife."

During my younger years in church, I'd hear people talk profusely about a "Proverbs 31 woman." My intrigue led me to begin reading the chapter; it opens with a mother's advice to her son. Similarly, the women in my life, such as my mother and grandmother, had their own methods of advice. My grandmother had a gift for coining phrases that still to this day remain with me. During my coming of age, she cautioned me to be mindful of the company kept. An encrypted message to prevent me from associating with the *wrong* type of woman—even though I still wasn't quite sure what specific qualities to look for.

I took a break from my search for a wife to focus on my business and my relationship with God. And honestly, that was the best thing I could have done. I learned how to project an aura of confidence, realizing that my preparation did not match my opportunities. I found myself in rooms where the interminable tabletops perfectly hid my jittering polished leather shoes.

I vividly remember enjoying a conversation in a West Coast fast-food joint. Both Erickajoy and I were visiting, her from

Maryland and I from Michigan. Her beautiful eyes, kind heart, and infectious smile captivated me. What started as a brief conversation evolved into a weeklong invitation to explore each other's personalities and how we were positioned for this very moment. We shared our desires, interests, and a mutual relationship with God—earnestly praying for one another while hundreds of miles apart, and eventually my friend became my prayer partner. She penned personal notes of encouragement that I would take with me as I traveled seeking career advancement opportunities. The letters became longer as our conversations became more personal. I had found someone who "opened her mouth with wisdom; and in her tongue was the law of kindness" (Proverbs 31:26).

After all the years of hearing and looking, I realized my friend and prayer partner was the same person who made my heart skip a beat. While the palpitations grew more frequent, I had only just begun to discover all the things she was capable of. Her academic journey not only landed her an amazing job, she had continued to study to become certified in life coaching. She was not selfish with what God had spoken to her and was uniquely positioned to unlock people's gifts and empower them to pursue their purpose.

As we continued to court, I had no idea that my friend, who had come into town to speak to a youth group, was going to run into both my mother and maternal grandmother. I should note that I come from a family of many strong women, none of whom will hesitate to protect me. Because Erickajoy and I were not officially dating, I had no reason to try and prepare her for this encounter. But it didn't take long for everyone she met to become enthralled with her helpful personality. "She stretcheth out her hand to the poor; yea, she reacheth forth her hands to the needy" (Proverbs 31:20).

Thankfully, I was not so blinded by my own career aspirations to miss this jewel who had already shown that she was clothed in strength and honor. Her actions toward others and earnest love for me are truly without comparison. I can still hear the ring of my grandmother's voice as she would call her name, accompanied by an undeniable smile. I had finally found a Proverbs 31 woman.

I have been blessed to witness everything she brings to the world throughout our sixteen years of marriage. While every chapter does not flatter me and some point out some challenges, it is all real-life anecdotes of a woman to whom I trust my heart. I have seen her awake at daybreak to pen prose and pray, seeking God about sharing her knowledge and challenges. I desire that each person who reads this book will hear her words of wisdom and use their God-given abilities to live out their calling.

I truly have found the love of my life and am excited to share her with you.

—Pastor John Daniels III

Acknowledgments

Fist order of business—appreciation: I have to take time and reflect on the contributors to this book. I want to reserve the space to acknowledge those who contributed in my life. Their investment in me is what has produced the beautiful return for this book to come to life.

First and foremost, my amazing husband. When we met, little did I know that he would be my life partner. I look back at pictures of us hanging out, and while visits and time together then only amounted to days, I now live a life where our time is slated for forever. He fills my life with creative exploration to discover life in new ways, challenge that develops me, laughter that brightens up my hardest days, and a presence that brings peace to my soul. Together we have the joy of raising a phenomenally gifted son who keeps me on my toes—from his insatiable curiosity for learning and his wit and savvy far beyond his years. Together as a family we believe in building legacy but building others. Our model of helping others in their growth is our foundational premise for service: you do, I help. www.youdoihelp.com

I knew what a great model for marriage was because of my parents. Their union of sixty-plus years was uncommon, but so was their commitment to each other. They taught my sister, brother, and me the root of healthy households being grounded in faith and service to one another. My mother, a giver whose well never runs dry; my father whose wisdom was a daily gift and treasure; an older sister who has a commitment to cover and protect; and a big brother with comedic wit and belief in his little sister all make for the gift of family that only God can offer.

My squad of women, fellow ladies of the gate who hold me up and hold me accountable, are the most precious set in my toolbox, as strong women of iron sharpening each other without selfish ambition. And the young women God continues to bring to my life keep me attentive to the life I live, so that I can be a responsible leader and resource for them.

My literary doula whose hands, heart, and hearing provided a guided journey for safe delivery of my first writing. Without her my pursuit and final product would not be the same. Which brings me to …

You. You have decided to pick up this book and join the journey. To connect with a new community. Your heart is why mine has been heavy and listening to God to write to you. Write for you and learn with you. So let's go take care of business.

Introduction

Welcome.

I recall a time when I was sitting on a plane, a delayed plane in fact, after waiting for a connecting flight to New York. It was rather late in the evening, I had worked a full day, and the little bambino I was carrying in my second trimester was tapping into my last bit of reserve energy. So, you would figure that a nice nap would have been calling my name right about that time of when my tank was on empty. But for some reason, sleep would not come. I felt a tapping, a nudge from my husband. And no, he wasn't the one sitting next to me. My plane neighbor was actually an unsuspecting stranger in the midst of reading his own book, who was looking rather intrigued at what I was furiously typing. (I must say, that is the same focused intrigue I look forward to seeing you experience as others watch you read and experience this journey.) But this tapping, as I mentioned, was from my husband, who was anxiously awaiting my arrival in New York City.

We had planned a family trip for the weekend, and I was en route to join the rest of the traveling crusaders. After a weekend adventure, I planned to head to Buffalo, New York, for my job, which kept me on the go. But again, I couldn't shake this tapping, this nudge.

I am sure you are asking why.

Well, Valentine's Day was the day before I left, and just a few days before then, my sweetie pie and I had talked about how we would celebrate this special day. A nice dinner away, cards, and gifts, of course, were the obvious options. But my husband was rather creative when I asked him what he wanted to get for Valentine's Day. His answer? "The first chapter of your book." Plain and direct. Simply stated, and purely challenged.

"My book, huh?" I asked. And with that, a simple, encouraging, sweet smile spread across his face. I think he realized he requested something that wasn't impossible, but something very particular and memorable, which is just how he can be at times.

And it hit me. My husband was very interested in seeing me used in the manner God has called me. He acknowledges my gifts and respects them. He also makes room for me when possible and removes barriers for me, even if that barrier is myself. He once asked me what keeps me from writing. I told him, "What if no one reads what I write?"

With wisdom and his signature wit, he replied, "Well, with them stuck in your head, no one sure can read them now."

He is not a perfect man but perfectly made for me. I've had a passion for writing for years, decades in fact. My dad was an author who could put pen to paper and so creatively flow with words that would paint the most precise picture you could close your eyes and imagine. He wrote for himself, his family, and his friends. But I never had the nerve and diligence to get to work. God strategically placed my husband in my life to see that I was called to a bigger audience, to allow God to speak to my heart, and to be a channel to share with others.

So, there I was. On a plane, working on my husband's gift. I had a few books on reserve in my head, but in line with his request, this was the perfect one for me to begin. I must be "the pen of a ready writer" (Psalm 45:1).

I offer you this, a gift from my heart inspired by the man who has my heart, prayerfully to touch your heart. It's so unselfish for my husband to make this request. To me, it means that it makes him happy and would put a smile on his face to see me grow and to see others grow. It's my prayer that God would use me to do just that. And if that's the case, suggest a friend pick up the book as well. That would keep the smile on my husband's face, I am sure.

Prep for the Learning Journey

This book is about taking care of business, a phrase we often use, but in this journey, I want to illuminate it a bit differently in context and outcomes. Many of us are used to to-do lists and checklists, and I admit, they keep me organized and accountable. Let's use the same approach for utilizing tools and models not just for activities but for personal awareness and growth. For every aspect of the 'business' we need to take care of, we are going to take an active approach of planning so we can get the job done. We must be as transparent as we can be, not for others to see right through us necessarily, but so that nothing gets in the way of us seeing ourselves. Wide-open space for God to review, revise, and rebuild us.

We will walk through aspects of ourselves—yes, time and focus to think of you first. Surprised? It's not self-serving but self-focused, so we can serve better. Remember that. God gives us an amazing playbook for our full lives, and in the space of relationships, He offers guidance, models, and encouragement for how we live. Let's map out a game plan that is biblically grounded, practical in nature, and a platform to yield good fruit in us, our relationships, our work, and our impact.

At the close of each chapter, we will pause and take a break to do a self-check to evaluate and take some time to plan, so we can take ownership of our role in striving to be a woman who takes care of business.

(Gentlemen, if you are reading this, don't create to-do lists for your mate. Instead, turn this into a prayer list and statements of belief of what you know God will manifest in your marriage. I ask for you to be open to the work required in each chapter as we build our business plans together.)

What are you going to do differently and look for with expectation of the change?

This self-check and planning time should be thoughtful, prayerful, and not driven by self-opinion. For that reason, use your resources: God's Word, the Holy Spirit, and godly counsel. If you are uncertain about those three resources, let's take care of that business up front.

The first resource is the Word.

I had a pastor who would always give us leaders a challenge when we prepared for a sermon, message, or any opportunity for instruction: "Put some Word on it." He stands by that so tough, he will often stop himself while teaching with the reminder to "Put some Word on it" for something he is clarifying for us. So, for each aspect, put some Word on it! There will be a space in your notes section or scriptural reference where you can capture Scriptures you find that are relevant and personal to you. And as you have your mind focused and determined to commit to this journey, God will honor that commitment and direct you to the Scriptures that are just for you! The Word must ground us. It is that by which we can see our God and our growth.

Which takes us to our second resource, the Holy Spirit.

I often see the Holy Spirit as a great messenger and conduit to God that enables me to enrich my relationship with Him. Capturing the Scriptures that I mentioned comes with the support of the Holy Spirit. He will do "special deliveries" for you. They will come through in a devotional, a song, a text from a solid friend. Keep your eyes, mind, and ears open for Him to speak as creatively as He desires to you. Catch everything He throws your way.

Our third resource is godly counsel. Don't assume this is your best friend. Or that it's your neighbor or coworker. What a blessing if that is your situation, but pay careful attention to whom you consider your ear and mouth for guidance and direction. That is critical! Psalm 1 gives us this reminder:

> Blessed is the man that walks not in the counsel of the ungodly, nor stands in the path of sinners, nor sits in the seat of the scornful. But his delight is in the law of the Lord; and in His law he meditates day and night. He shall be like a tree planted by the rivers of water, that brings forth its fruit in its season; whose leaf also shall not wither; and whatever he does shall prosper. (Psalm 1:1–3)

To be blessed is a state of favor. It is a position that God allows you to possess, as a matter of His outpouring. It's not situational but sustainable and requires a "maintenance fee" on our part. We must pay the cost of prayer, seek the Lord, put Him first, and recognize and respect that He is Lord—and live a life that demonstrates His lordship in our life. Then we can say humbly, not with righteous indignation, that we are blessed. Now, *that's* a position I want to be in.

So my godly counsel that I seek should not be from those who are not following the Lord (the ungodly), nor should I march in tune with the world, their ways and suggestions (stand in the way of sinners) or allow myself to be fed by negativity or criticizers (sit in the seat of the scornful). The Word is the base. That is the source.

And oh, the benefits!

Have you ever seen a tree that had an unlimited supply of water (planted right by the rivers of water)? There is no telling what it can produce if it positions itself right near the source of provision. But back up a minute; the tree is planted, which means it can't be moved. It is rooted to weather whatever comes. Trust me, in the years of marriage, if I could tell you the weather forecasts that I have seen and the storms experienced! Yet somehow, though the forecast was grim and sometimes treacherous, my marriage is still standing! Both my husband and I are blessed to say that our parents have weathered over 100 years collectively with the same mate from day one. And they have been honest enough with us to share some of their past weather forecasts. *But*, their marriages have remained, and may I say that fruit has been abundant with offspring, success, legacy, and increase. So, do you believe this tree planting notion will work?

We will follow the same format for the close of each of our chapters. Seeking God's guidance, each time we need to take care of business, we will personally reflect and record:

- My **ASK**. "What specific question(s) do I need to ask God?"

  Write it down so you know exactly what you are petitioning Him for and what you can look back and specifically give Him thanks for.

- God's **ANSWER**. "What do I hear God saying in response to my question?"

  Don't rush this step, and don't restrict God on how He answers. It can be a song, a Scripture that comes to mind, a word from a trusted friend, a commercial that sparks a new revelation. Remember God has no limits, so don't limit Him; just listen with expectation.

- My **ASSIGNMENT**. "What do I do with what God said? What do I need to do differently? What bold move or courageous step do I need to take? What change of direction do I need to make?"

  This stage is where we get to put our new insight into action. In each chapter, you will be building your game plan, which will also serve as your accountability plan and praise report!

- God's **ASSURANCE**. "What does God's Word say to me?"

  Search for Scriptures that will remind you of God's promise and His instruction. If you feel led to pray more, find Scriptures on prayer. If God wants you to change your circle of friends and influencers, look up Scriptures on the traits of a good friend. God will continue to comfort you in knowing He is with you along the way and has promises for you.

This is our business plan mapped out for us. At the close of each chapter, you should not only read, consume, experience, and seek God's direction, but you should also journal it. Write it down and make it plain. Set yourself up for the script that will be your testimony of overcoming and success.

Keep moving chapter by chapter while you are taking care of business, and do the work chapter by chapter. By the time we get to the close of this journey, we are positioned to look back and ask ourselves, *How did I change in this process and how did my marriage change?* This is your toolkit that you can always go back to. When an issue arises, you will know you have a resource and a record of learning to pull from and apply for any situation. There will be plenty of space in the book for you to keep all your discoveries, insights, and more together. Keep it all in the book. It's yours!

CHAPTER 1

∼⁓∼

MY RATIONALE

Taking Care of Business While My Husband Is at the Gate—long title, but I hope it sticks with you. This book came to mind quite some time ago—in fact, in my singleness, and before I even knew my husband, which is vital. The Lord impressed upon me in my time of preparation *for* marriage that I had a gift ahead *in* marriage, which I was truly looking forward to, but a responsibility would come with it. Don't get me wrong, I was guilty of daydreaming of my perfect wedding day, and occasionally—okay, I admit—*daily* found myself visited by thoughts of being swept away by a Prince Charming. But the Holy Spirit would grab me by my coattails in my drifting and ground me to keep me balanced, never to erase the dream or have me dismayed that it wouldn't happen, but developing a solid understanding and appreciation that for every prince, there should be an amazing princess. And I wanted to get ready for that role.

I felt the Lord impressing upon me to prepare for work ahead. I had many key people in my life, including my parents, pastor, mentors, and friends, tell me that in praying for me, they felt the strong sense that I would in some way be "hitting the ground running" when it came to marriage. Along with the new joy and excitement of being a newlywed, they felt that the opportunities to be loved and, in turn, serve others in love would come swiftly. Learning that God gives a gift of love in marriage and that gift should be given to others helped shaped my expectations of how I would step into this commitment.

I was always very active in ministry since I was a child, in some form or fashion, so why would I expect things to change? I agreed with the "cloud of witnesses" that God placed in my life that my soulmate would have the same history and passion of being a diligent worker, someone who filled himself up to pour into others. It only made sense that if He wired the two of us that way, we would continue to remain active, and whatever energy God gave us in our wiring would be used to energize and empower others.

So, back to "the gate." Along with most of the Christian population of single women, I have prayed, read, studied, memorized, and treated Proverbs 31 like a job description. Spoiler alert! In an upcoming chapter, we will dig into more of what that job description fully entails. But at a high level, this Proverbs 31 woman would be my profile to model myself after. The sewing, the selling, getting up with the roosters, cleaning, etc., I had to admit, didn't quite seem to fit with my schedule or my vision for myself. But hey, I wanted a good man, who I assumed was in search of a good woman with this Proverbs resume, so I was up for the challenge.

But one day, a verse stuck out to me: "Her husband is known in the gates, when he sits among the elders of the land" (Proverbs 31:23). I couldn't divert my attention from it.

I started to ask myself, *Why is this even mentioned?* God always speaks with intention, and I wanted to understand more. *Where is this gate? What is this gate?* What did it all mean? I knew the focus in that passage of Scripture was an instructional piece of wisdom regarding the character and capacity of an ideal godly woman. Still, I saw that part of who she is had something to do with whom she is connected to. It speaks of her husband at this gate. So with the historically inquisitive side of me that I inherited from my father, I started searching for the meaning of "the gate."

It turns out that the gate was a place of prominence for the men in the city. It wasn't just a hangout spot for the fellas to gather in the town square. It was a convening of high intellectual discussion, informative debate, and sharing of wisdom. It was a learning place, and those who were in attendance were part of a special crowd. The gate was a place where courts of justice were kept, key decisions made, contracts negotiated, businesses established, and advancement was being designed for the city. A place like that, with a powerful atmosphere like that, meant it took people who could bring that ability and ambience with them to bring it all to life.

The gate itself physically had no particular significance outside of it being in a visible place. It was more about what happened there at the gate and the character of those who were invited and welcomed to be there. For this man to be known at the gate meant he had a seat in a place that was notable. A man notably honored in his community honors his wife as noted in verse 29: "Many daughters have done virtuously, but thou excellest them all." It was an honor to even be at the gate—let alone for him to use his prominence to acknowledge the prominence of his wife in his home so unselfishly. That says something pretty amazing to me about this couple.

A look at a power household like that drew me in, and the scene impacted my personal development plan. I saw a husband who was not only a knight in shining armor but a prince of some sort. Not of money, wealth or fame, but of notoriety, influence, and presence. A man who could command attention with his thoughts and careful intentional speech. A man whose wisdom was sought after and whose counsel was solicited by others. A man who ...

Wait a minute! Am I up for this *challenge?* I mean, I could hold my own, but this was no average guy I was to be expecting. Then the same grounding Holy Spirit caught me and reminded me that I was no average woman myself because of the God that I called Lord and who answered me as His own daughter. He took me back to my favorite verse, which has been my life verse for decades. "I have been crucified with Christ, it is no longer I who live, but Christ lives in me. And the life which I now live in the flesh, I live by faith in the Son of God who loved me and gave Himself for me" (Galatians 2:20). So this amazing marriage God has in store for me, I will live out with this same faith and know that God has a purpose and a plan. *Whew, that took a load off my shoulders* ... and I was back to working on getting ready for my man at the gate.

It's incredible how, looking ahead, I see parts of my husband in what God has shown me in the past. Now, I am not saying my husband is the head of the gate—yet (smile). But he has a clear seat there. And I say that as a reminder to you. As you progress through this book, it's not a matter of what seat or position your husband holds now. It is a matter of his calling to a place to serve and lead. Remember, this leading is not confined to specific titles or positions the way we traditionally think of them, but refers to positions of influence. As creative as God is in making us, He is as creative at making ways for us to lead, avenues for us to influence, and opportunities for us to impact others. So keep a watchful, prayerful eye on the current gate or the gate ahead that God is shaping and securing for the seat he wants your loved one to occupy.

This prayerful guarding and watching is a strong duty for those whose mates are already positioned, those who may not yet be at the gate, or even those who were once there and need to return. We as women have the responsibility to see our husbands how God made them and where God sees them, even if it's not in the flesh right now. My husband is a young man who has much that God has yet for him to accomplish. But with the fruit that I already see in his life, his passion, and commitment to the Lord, and the promises that God shared with me concerning him, I am proud to say he is at the gate. That confident acknowledgment needs to not only be our declaration but also our demonstration so much so that our actions resemble a woman proud to be connected to a man of impact.

Where does that leave us then? Ready for the rationale of this learning journey together? It means we must take care of business while our man is at the gate. He is there with a freedom to know that all is well at home, spiritually, physically, financially, and emotionally. For him to rest assured there, and grow and impact others at the gate, we need to attend to some business back home. I am in no regard suggesting we take over and lead things; that would be contradictory to God's plan and order. But there are some things of the physical home, our dwelling place of a home, and the emotional "home" of our marriage and the "home" of our heart and character that we must take care of. As the chapters advance, we will create a TCB list, a "Taking Care of Business" list, of what matters we need to attend to, along with God's direction on how to be successful at it. They will cause us to look at our surroundings and ourselves, but it's all for the Savior.

Taking Care of Business (TCB) #1: Knowing My Rationale

TCB #1: I have shared my rationale for delivering this book to you. Now I want you to take some dedicated time and prayerfully seek God on your decision to dig into this book and what you want to get out of this journey. Consider what intrigued you and use that to understand how your rationale will continue to inspire you.

My **ASK**. "What specific question(s) do I need to ask God?"

God's **ANSWER**. "What do I hear God saying in response to my question?"

My **ASSIGNMENT**. "What do I do with what God said? What do I need to do differently? What bold move or courageous step do I need to take? What change of direction do I need to make?"

God's **ASSURANCE**. "What does God's Word say to me?"

_____

_____

_____

_____

CHAPTER 2

⁓⁓⁓

MY REALITY

Okay, before we even begin, let me be transparent from the start. I am going to pose a question that I am assuming may be a popular question based on the thoughts that have passed through my own mind and those that have been passed along from the number of women I have been in dialogue with in preparation for and creation of this book: Is the Proverbs woman realistic in today's world?

Just think with me for a minute. How many times have you either passed a bookshelf, perused the internet, or listened in on a discussion around the ideal godly woman—this woman with all her amazing ability to take on the world—only to put down the book, decide not to download the article, or sit in a seat of doubt. Did you wonder, *How in the world is this type of feat even practical today? Is there a contemporary version of this phenomenal woman? Am I seeking something attainable?*

I want to propose to you that it is both practical and attainable. One thing that hit me was that the world, and our personal habitation in it, is nothing that has taken God by surprise. He had this all on His radar screen from the day you were born. He is the master pilot who attends to everything on His radar, guiding and navigating through and past turbulence and storms if we don't try to take over the wheel.

Let me be clear up front. You have a friend with a pen—an author who has at the forefront of her mind the pervasive concern, *How can I become a Proverbs 31 woman without trying to take over the wheel?* As your friend with a pen, my aim is to share with you the unadulterated story, empathizing right along with you on the pressing challenges, seemingly insurmountable demands, and the big and small hands that pull at you every day.

Let me give you a peek inside of the life of Erickajoy. I will start inside out. I am the youngest of three children. My siblings are amazing. All of us partnered to take care of my mom after my father's passing. My mom settled in to live with me, so she has become my travel and hangout partner everywhere we go. You can find this all-white-haired woman, nearly eighty years old, on a sled in the winter or the back of a Harley in the summer. I do my best to make sure that until God calls her home she is able to live her best life.

My teammates at home include my son and my husband. My guys are the ones who bring me joy and are my determination for working hard and my company when it's time to play hard.

It is no small feat having a husband, John III, who is at the gate with a few hats as a pastor, community leader, and entrepreneur. As unique as God made him is as unique as God made me for him. We have shared goals and dreams yet distinct paths and callings to serve others. He runs a nonprofit organization that provides career, social, and educational development and experiences for young men. I have the honor of supporting him, his dreams, and his work by offering my skills and expertise to his organization. And though at times it feels like I have 150 plus young men to invest in, my first and only son is my other special guy at home.

My husband's namesake, John IV, is a precocious, curious, creative young man with an old soul. He is a creative and the founder and owner of a greeting card business that he started at the age of eight. He loves financial investing and travel and serves as the expert of both in the house.

My guys are my fuel of inspiration to do what I do as a corporate executive. The hours are long, the work is intense, but I know I am called to do what I do. Being responsible for people and proven results is anchored in my purpose. I am grateful that God has given me the gifts and the heart to serve and to do so not only in my professional seat but the open doors where he calls me to lead. That includes serving on boards, mentoring young women, serving as a college instructor, and networking with leaders in my community.

Whew! Wait, how in the world do I find time to be a Proverbs 31 woman? I know I am not the only one with a whirlwind of duties like this. In respect of my life and schedule being full, I know I am not alone. That's a reassurance.

The wonderful thing is you are not alone. Though it may sometimes feel as if you are the only one in your family, circle of friends, or even area code who has to manage the weight you do, you are not alone. You are not the only one with the litany of to-dos including picking up the kids and putting down your own preferences, coordinating schedules in the house that don't offer any "me time," managing the bills, and daydreaming about hiring a gardener one day who could plant some trees that yield cash. At the end of the day, your bubble bath and bed are relentlessly calling your name as if you abandoned them, but the voices of your family and friends seem to drown them out and end up winning in the end.

So, let's take this journey together. Why? Why take on the challenge? Because I truly believe God has trusted you to do so. The very reason you are reading this book is because you have or desire to have a husband at the gate, you recognize that comes with great responsibility, and you know you need more. Don't get me wrong, I am not the "more" in your life, just a fellow sojourner on this road of responsibility who wants to share the more she has learned along the way and the wonderful lessons God has downloaded to me. I am simply choosing to click my spiritual save button and share the great word with my network.

*   *   *

This great Word came alive for me. I didn't need to look up and see how I would make time to be this Proverbs 31 woman. I had to open my eyes and see the reality of her description become my own. The verses in Proverbs 31 were not restricted to one character, but a framework for God to demonstrate how creative He is at bringing the persona to life in countless women for countless ages.

Let me help you see what God helped me see as he pulled back the veil to reveal me on the stage of a virtuous woman.

- "The heart of her husband safely trusts her" (v. 11). He trusts my judgment with how I spend our money.
- "She does him good and not evil" (v. 12). I want the best for his business and the countless people he serves. I will support his dreams.

- "She seeks wool … and willingly works with her hands" (v. 13). I work to bring vibrancy and change by building strategies, building relationships, and identifying people who are the fabric of the community.
- "She brings her food from afar" (v. 14). I always make sure my family is well fed.
- "She also rises while it is yet night" (v. 15). My late night tasks make sure my family is set for the next day.
- "She considers a field and buys it" (v. 16). My considerations include investing in the stock market, building a 401(k), and naming my son and husband as beneficiaries on my benefits.
- "She strengthens her arms" (v. 17). I remain physically active and healthy to be in the best condition to take care of my family.
- "She perceives that her merchandise is good" (v. 18). I am proud of the creative ideas, projects, and strategies God gives me.
- "Her hand holds the spindle" (v. 19). I am committed and diligent to the work I do for and with my family.
- "She reaches out her hands to the needy" (v. 20). I support my husband in ministry and am a faithful tither and financial supporter.
- "Her household is clothed with scarlet" (v. 21). God has given me the gift of frugality and favor in shopping for the best.
- "Her clothing is fine linen and purple" (v. 22). I carry myself well wherever I go.
- "Her husband is known in the gates" (v. 23). God has gifted me to support a leader.

- "She makes linen garments and sells them" (v. 24). I am a good steward of the resources God places in our house.
- "Strength and honor are her clothing" (v. 25). My character is one of my best features.
- "She opens her mouth with wisdom" (v. 26). I take care in choosing my words so they bring life.
- "She does not eat the bread of idleness" (v. 27). Laziness for me is not an option.

We can make the ideal become real in our lives. Read the Scripture as your script, and let God put you on the stage. "And blessed is she that believed: for there shall be a performance of those things which were told her from the Lord" (Luke 1:45). Know your current reality and embrace it. We may need to work on more scenes, but He is the writer and producer of this great performance. So, take a deep breath, get a pen and journal with a lot of pages, settle in, and let's take care of business.

TCB #2: Knowing My Reality

Take time to think of your current reality. What responsibilities do you currently have on your plate? Of those, which have you confirmed with God should really be there?

My **ASK**. "What specific question(s) do I need to ask God?"

God's **ANSWER**. "What do I hear God saying in response to my question?"

My **ASSIGNMENT**. "What do I do with what God said? What do I need to do differently? What bold move or courageous step do I need to take? What change of direction do I need to make?"

God's **ASSURANCE**. "What does God's Word say to me?"

_____

_____

_____

_____

_____

_____

_____

_____

_____

_____

_____

_____

_____

_____

_____

_____

_____

_____

_____

CHAPTER 3

~~~

MY ROLE

One thing God has convicted me of as He works through me to serve others is the need for transparency. One of my mentors once said, "Sometimes more is learned that is caught rather than what is taught." In other words, some of the best life lessons happen through living the practical application and understanding that come from the "classroom" of life, when someone can courageously let you in to peek at more than the surface and more than just what is good. I strive to be a transparent follower of Christ and a transparent leader for Him. I must always look at myself through transparency first, so let me make that same offer in our learning journey together.

There was a time when I was entertaining a chance to make a career move, shifting industries from corrections to manufacturing. It was a significant shift for me, but as I look back, it was all part of God's developing me for the steps He had ahead for me. Candidly, at the time I didn't hold on to the assurance of God's strategic chess moves in my mind; but instead, that valuable assurance was clouded with self-doubt and fear. I came across a job description for a role with a global company that, at the core of the job, was aligned with my skillset at the time. But the scope and reach of the role seemed more like a future opportunity, and I got in my own way by thinking my current abilities at the time had to be my forever achievements. Reading the description, I saw that it spoke about more strategic-level thinking, influencing across states without positional authority, taking on new leadership challenges, and connecting with stakeholders internally and externally. That was a lot more than I had experienced before, but thank God that He planted a seed of curiosity that intrigued me and that He gifted me with a mentor who inspired me.

Now, as I think about it, we could almost use the duties in that job description to explain marriage as well. And many of us enter that "job" of wife sometimes doubtful of the expectations of the role. So, let me offer some mentoring advice: Think of what you can do, then think of what you can do.

I know I repeated myself, but we have to think of what we can currently do and *also* think of what we can do in the future. Hold to the promise of Philippians 4:13: "I *can* do all things through Christ which strengthens me." So, hold on to that strength and can-do mentality as we dive into the role of this woman married to the man at the gate.

Let's look at the overarching role, and then we will get to the responsibilities in that role. A role is a specific position you are in, and the responsibilities are the expectations of you in that role. Knowing your assignment up front clearly is key, as it provides the overarching, long-term view of who you are to be in your relationship. See your position as being transformational in your marriage and not just transactional. This higher-level view enables you to take an aerial peek of how God has positioned you. At times, you may delegate responsibilities, but you cannot relinquish your role as a wife. Let's take, for example, the duty of ensuring your family is fed. You can pick up food from a friend or restaurant, and while you didn't cook the meal yourself, you were certain that the family had what it needed. There are things that you don't necessarily have to do yourself, but you have to ensure it's done.

As you go through seasons independently and together, your scope may broaden or narrow, your tasks may shift or evolve, but your role remains constant. Your nicknames may come and go, but you are stepping into the confirmed seat of wife, a wife of a man at the gate. Own your role. Embrace your role. And continually seek God's guidance to understand your role fully.

So, as I go back to my career shift, while the narrative at the top of the job description intrigued me, the responsibilities scared me. Sounds like a marriage, right? The story that is advertised or even imagined in our own heads is of the man who sweeps us off our feet. For this role we get to step in to be adored, loved, admired, pampered, taken care of, delighted, accompanied, rescued from loneliness, paid attention to, respected, treated, and whisked away into happily ever after. That grabs our attention, along with the desire to say swiftly, *Sign me up!* But if you're honest, like I was with myself, the duties will make you pause a little bit.

Take any time you have been to a wedding with traditional vows. The bride has to answer the questions. Imagine this in her mind:

I … take you … to be my husband (*Yes, I have been waiting!*)
to have and to hold (*Yes, you are all mine.*)
from this day forward (*We get to grow old together.*)
for better (*Absolutely!*)
for worse (*Hmm …*)
for richer (*Sounds good!*)

for poorer (*Well, hope we don't get there.*)
in sickness and in health (*Let's hope for all health.*)
to love and to cherish (*I truly do.*)
to obey (*Well, wait a minute ...*)
till death us do part (*I sure will try.*)

I say that jokingly, but it's a real gut check to understand the godly commitment of marriage and all that comes with it. But if God set you up, God's got the setup for you, for an amazingly successful marriage. And God being the spark is sure to keep the right kind of fire. So let's get confident in our role so we can get comfortable with our responsibilities. There is a job God has called me into and called you into—a specific assignment for a specific man that He would gift to us in our lives, and that together, our work would have a greater impact than we could imagine.

In my career, not only have I had to read job roles and descriptions but I have also had to write them and guide others to do the same. So let me offer some support as I want you to do the same. If I can share an approach and some thoughts for you to consider, this chapter's TCB list will be about understanding and articulating your role. For our purposes, we will look at the job title and the job summary to help us understand our role. Let's look first at the practical model of doing this then we will apply it for our context.

One thing many human resource professionals do before designing a job is to do a job analysis. The analysis involves gathering information and insight about the job to develop the best profile. This data collection can be done through steps like interviewing people in the position or similar jobs, observing how tasks are done in that job, and collecting data from other resources to learn as much about the background and impact of the job. I invite you to do to the same. Don't approach this lightly, and you don't have to learn alone. Of course, start with the Word to get God's background, find individuals with solid marriages or those who have learned from marriages that needed to be strengthened, and observe those who do this job well. Your personal work to do the analysis will prepare you for the best profile, and you will see the distinction of how unique you should be in your marriage.

Key Traits of a Job Title and Summary

Job titles should:

- be specific and accurate to who you are called to be.
- draw you in, honor God, and align with the impact you have on your husband.

Job summaries should:

- be strong and solid.
- give a high-level view of what is distinct about this position you have been placed in.
- call out what is distinct and unique.
- reflect your "brand" as an individual and as a partner in a strong marriage.
- include the culture or the tone of your marriage.
- be indicative of what brings you two together in a unique way.

- describe what your marriage will impact and deliver because the two of you are together.
- offer the goals you want to achieve in this position.
- be an introduction, setting up the stage for the job responsibilities.

Let me offer you mine as an example to start your thinking.

Job Title: John's Joy

For me, this is a play on our names. My father named me Erickajoy. Being a miracle baby for my parents, I do believe they were determined that I would be a vessel of joy. When I got married, my dad entrusted my husband with taking care of me, so to me, I am his in name and what I offer to him. My role is to bring joy to my husband—joy and not despair, being an asset and not a liability.

Job Summary:

John's Joy will join an entity that has been established as a creative hub for identifying and developing individuals, families, and communities. She will have the honor of serving in a collaborative role of leadership, providing support through her distinct gifts, skills, and experience that are complementary to the standing capability set in the entity. She will be expected to bring strategic thinking, problem-solving, instruction, and wisdom. The culture is fast paced, and often, because the entity is one of innovation, there are seasons of ambiguity and the need for agility. Given the service component, it is also highly externally facing, so she can serve well with her strong relationship-building skills. In this role, together, the entity will be able to build the confidence, capability, and capacity of others, for long-term results, impact, and reach. There is an aspect of travel associated with the role, nationally and internationally. The entity is positioned for legacy, and all work will contribute to a sustainable model for years to come.

This summary excites me and scares me, but I know it's the position God has called me to. There is an old hymn that stands out to me as a banner reminder of my *why*—"A Charge to Keep I Have." It is an old hymn written by Charles Wesley (1707–1788). The lyrics speak to the call each believer has to evangelize. But whenever I feel a press, a call from God explicitly for my diligent action, this hymn speaks to me. It's not written as a love song, but for me, it speaks to the love I have for God and the love I have for my husband in understanding the role I have in his life, is a role God has called me to.

A Charge to Keep I Have

A charge to keep I have,
A God to glorify;
A never dying soul to save,
And fit it for the sky.

To serve the present age,
My calling to fulfill:
O may it all my powers engage,
To do my Master's will!

Arm me with jealous care,
As in thy sight to live;

44

And O, thy servant, Lord, prepare,
A strict account to give!

Help me to watch and pray,
And on thyself rely;
By faith assured I will obey,
For I shall never die.

A charge is not a slight suggestion but a strong statement of called-out responsibility. That is how the Lord wants us to see marriage! It's not just a nice thing to have someone to keep you warm, send you flowers, and whisper sweet nothings in your ear. Though I do love all those perks and more! But even more, it is an experience of expected commitment to ultimately serve God in ways He presents and unfolds along the way. It is *He* that must be glorified in our marriage, in what we do together. Now don't get me wrong, there are wonderful benefits and highlights in this thing called marriage. But some responsibilities come with the territory, and while there are aspects in marriage that give us some joy, our personal enjoyment is not the goal. Hate to break it to you. The *ultimate* goal is for us to represent the model of the church—the bride (His church) and the Bridegroom (*Christ*)!—and through our representation, to let the world see God's true intention of love and service. Yes, you get to play a part in the whole performance!

TCB #3: Knowing my Role

I want you to take some dedicated time and prayerfully seek God on your specific role. Part of your assignment is to pen your role description. God is the author; your job is simply to be the scribe. You will want to capture the high-level, aerial view of your transformational job. Don't speak to your duties just yet, but your role.

My **ASK**. "What specific question(s) do I need to ask God?"

God's **ANSWER**. "What do I hear God saying in response to my question?"

My **ASSIGNMENT**. "What do I do with what God said? What do I need to do differently? What bold move or courageous step do I need to take? What change of direction do I need to make?"

God's **ASSURANCE**. "What does God's Word say to me?"

_____

_____

_____

_____

_____

_____

_____

_____

CHAPTER 4

~~~

MY RESPONSIBILITIES

When I was single and desiring to be married, I had a list of duties in mind that I thought would be my responsibility as a wife. It included everything from the usual: be attractive to and for him, be a good listener, be a good communicator, be available for him emotionally and physically, be a woman of integrity, be a good mother, be a good steward of our finances, and more. And yes, those were all key. But it was after I got married that I realized some key aspects of all those expectations. I had to understand *why* I had to be *who* God was looking for me to be for my spouse.

Let's go back to that "charge" we talked about earlier. The charge to keep that *you* have is described in the words you captured about your role. It's personal. That is *why* you were recruited for this specific position, for a unique opportunity and countless blessings you will enjoy in the experience of marriage that you can't even imagine. And if I continue with this notion of being recruited, it takes me back to my last career shift: a new industry, a new trade, a new level of leadership—all more than I could imagine for myself, candidly. To top it all off, they reached out to me. Something about me was intriguing enough for the organization to seek me out. They ironically saw something in me beyond what I could see in myself.

Isn't that like God? He will seek you out and set you up for your "next," and often that "next" comes with responsibilities and abilities we may think are beyond us. Let's celebrate the fact that our God sees the amazingness He placed in us above the apprehensions we hold for ourselves. And the Word is true as it tells us, "He who finds a wife finds a good thing. And obtains favor from the Lord. (Proverbs 18:22) You are God's good thing, and when we make room for Him, He is the master recruiter and will draw the best person, who becomes our connection to find success in and with.

Remember this: remarkable marriages don't happen by happenstance but because of intention and determination. God begins the journey of intention for us to see the gifts inside of us, and we then own the duty of seeking, understanding, and seizing the opportunities for those gifts to come alive and flourish. We have *got to* see our part in this, and we do so by recognizing the responsibility that we first commit ourselves to the charge. Hold that charge close to your heart, so much that it beats with it in harmony. That charge should drive you, encourage you, sustain you, fuel you, invigorate you, remind you, and constrain you. Because yes, it's not always going to be your number one desire. Can we be honest here? You are not always going to feel like serving, loving, attending to, encouraging, and "all other duties as assigned" to and for your mate. But your commitment to your charge will give you such a powerful "nevertheless spirit" and attitude that you will operate with a peace that passes your own understanding.

So, let's go back to your role. That role and charge come with very specific responsibilities. I want to switch our thinking to be less tactical, though, for a moment and get to the heart of what I am responsible for. Then the actual activities will be more apparent, and we can build out the checklists we love to make.

I feel I am responsible for many things in my marriage, but let's just walk through a few. I feel responsible for the safekeeping of my husband's fears. Big one, right! But I do think that part of being his helpmeet means I should offer the environment and myself as a safe place for him to be vulnerable. This is particularly important for those men who are leading at the gate.

In my career, I have had the responsibility to do executive coaching in formal and informal settings. One main observation that influenced how I engaged with leaders is that they live their lives in a fishbowl: Everyone watching. Everyone critiquing. Everyone commenting. Yet, not everyone always applauding. Leadership comes with this space of constant view, and my coaching style had to be one of protected space. It had to be a place where the only eyes that mattered were the ones of the leader, for time, for reflection and self-awareness. That is how true growth happens. When leaders got to a place where they could trust me, they told me more, shared more than expected, and allowed themselves to be vulnerable. That vulnerability led to the perfect garden to plant seeds of candid recognition and acceptance for self-improvement, yielding fruit of growth and development.

That, my friends, is my responsibility for my husband. I need to set a garden where he knows he is safe to share. It is my responsibility to ensure that this safe place is so well established for him, that he may find assurance that it's a protected place where some little birdie will not take his seeds of what he has shared and carry them off somewhere through damaging gossip; rather, the roots he plants of improvement,

I will meticulously water with care, and the resulting harvest of his personal growth I will celebrate with him and not offer to others.

That place of responsibility, in my mind, is his home base that prepares him for the next victory he has to take on. Coming out, he can confidently return to his place of prominence, his seat of decision-making, and find that he is stronger and wiser because he had a safe place to reflect, revise, and reset. While usually surrounded by many, he found solace and support at home base where he had an audience of only two, where his God and his wife were there to support the necessary moments of vulnerability that leaders go through. I can only imagine him at the gate when the day gets challenging, feeling assured that he has a garden back home to return to for any weed pulling, pruning, and reseeding so he can get strong and get back to the gate. This cycle of planting, watering, and harvesting is the model for his growth where I see my responsibility laid out.

I must admit, it takes work. Taking on the project of gardening my front yard was one adventure that was more than I had expected. I had big dreams of this beautifully colored, massive front yard that was curb-appeal ready. I went off to not only one or two but five garden stores to collect and amass an arrangement of various plants and flowers that were going to come home with me to make my abode even more dazzling. And I didn't stop there. I had gone online and ordered the tools, the natural sprays, the hoses, the sprinklers, the garden gloves, and even a new pair of garden clogs as, of course, I wanted to be the cute gardener. My first few weeks out, I had what I thought was a routine, a loose cadence of checking on my garden but disappointed that I was not seeing the results

I was hoping for. The unfortunate problem was my investment was mismatched.

The leaves were drooping, the buds were slow, and the roots were dry—all because I invested more time in the preparation and dreams of the garden than I did in the actual work and effort. If only I had cared for the garden more than I commented on it. If only I had watered more than I walked by it. If only I had put my hands to work more than I put my hopes to just wishing it would work out. Imagine that garden as your marriage.

I am glad to share that a turnaround occurred when I recognized I wasn't taking care of my responsibilities. I was wise enough to ask for help from some family garden gurus, but they were careful to provide support without removing responsibility. They took the time to teach me, model for me, and even spend time in the garden with me. But it was my duty to take on because it was my dream. My mind and actions shifted, and my comments turned to genuine care with me listening intently to the wise counsel on how to grow my garden. My walks past the garden were replaced by stepping into the garden, not afraid to get sweaty and dirty but getting to know the terrain I was responsible for. And my hands did the work I had recklessly left undone. The result was new buds on the flowers, new height on the stems, more color and vibrancy, and it was less about curb appeal for others than the satisfaction of the fruit of my work and the smile on my husband's face as a bonus.

I dare say there is a certain curb appeal to marriage. But our intention for drawing the look of those around us should not be one of selfish gain but for onlookers to see God at work in a fruitful marriage. So when they look and see the fruit of your labor, the vibrancy results from good "marriage gardening" steps. Where we shift our minds, actions, and comments about our marriage and replace those things by care and attention to our mate. This comes out through our listening, understanding his needs, learning how he grows, and knowing what's best for him to thrive. Know if you have a sun or shade partner—does he flourish in the light or is he a low-key kind of guy—and support whatever style he is. Step into situations instead of just walking by. Take the time to understand the roots of his fears, his apprehensions, his concerns. Water his heart when sometimes that comes through heartfelt tears to God on his behalf. And do not avoid the job of the work, the labor, and the responsibilities.

So that is how my responsibility to safe keep my husband's fears translates to actual actions I take as a wife. I am proud to see my garden out front. It has become quite an honor for me to watch it grow. I get excited to add new aspects to my garden, and even though I still seek help, which is not only more than fine, but wise, I have taken ownership of my duties. Just like my marriage. I still seek godly counsel so that I can do my best with being a fruit-bearing, blossoming wife and remain determined to personally grow, support my husband's growth, and delight in the growth of our marriage.

TCB #4: Knowing My Responsibilities

Now it's your turn. I want you to take some dedicated time and prayerfully seek God on your responsibilities—those expectations that bring your job summary to life. Remember, God is the author; your job is simply to be the scribe. Ask God to show you one thing you are "responsible for" for your husband. And then ask God to illuminate how you can bring that responsibility to life.

My **ASK**. "What specific question(s) do I need to ask God?"

God's **ANSWER**. "What do I hear God saying in response to my question?"

My **ASSIGNMENT**. "What do I do with what God said? What do I need to do differently? What bold move or courageous step do I need to take? What change of direction do I need to make?"

God's **ASSURANCE**. "What does God's Word say to me?"

_____

_____

_____

_____

_____

_____

_____

_____

_____

_____

_____

CHAPTER 5

MY REPUTATION

When I was getting ready to go away to college, I had the fortunate experience of spending some valuable time with my godmother on weekends. I would go to her house under the guise of needing to get my hair done, but as I look back, I see what she was helping to style was my character and mindset as a holy young lady. My godmother had a way with hair and always had me looking fabulous, but the challenges she gave me, the wisdom she imparted, and the knowledge she passed on to me all helped with the true beauty that God wanted to see in me.

One of the fundamental things I remember her telling me was "Your reputation is golden." It was up to me to keep it shining or willingly allow it to pass through the hands of others for it to be subject to tarnish. At the time, I didn't fully understand why it was so critical, but as I got older, I saw how one's reputation could spread for miles, across many circles, and last for years. I just had enough sense at the time to listen to a wise woman and take caution.

I came to understand the focus she was advising me regarding being a young woman of God. There is a level of holiness that God expects and a demonstration He looks for us to give. As the old folk say, "Show some sign." I learned to strive to make sure that my walk was matching my talk. I couldn't say one thing on one side of campus and have another thing spoken about me on the other side of campus. Authenticity and authenticity to a high standard was a necessity.

So, let's build upon these thoughts: a standard, holiness, authenticity, and reputation. They are building blocks and can lead to a strong fortress or a tower of unstable doom. Now, which would you prefer be said of your household?

Back to the building blocks.

The Standard

God has set a standard for us for holy living. There is no believer, woman or man, who can say that they are not aware that a standard exists, but how aware are we of how we line up with it? In my role at work, I hold people accountable for poor performance on the job. When I work with an individual manager who is frustrated with an employee—fed up that they are exhibiting a bad attitude, not meeting deadlines, delivering shoddy results, and the manager is at a breaking point—they come to me. "EJ, I am ready to fire this team member!"

I hear them out, pause, and ask them one critical question, "Did you lay out the expectations?"

Too often, unfortunately, I get a deer-in-the-headlights reaction. "They should know better."

But I cannot represent my company and allow a manager to release someone without expectations being clear. I often have to send them on their way to deliver not a termination notice but a coaching plan to lay out clear expectations. Just like our Father, who would rather develop us than dismiss us.

I am so glad God is not quick to fire us! On many occasions, my performance has been less than desirable, but He sends me off with the Holy Spirit to coach me and takes me back to the Word where the expectations are laid out. Then the ball is in my court to live up to the standards God has set for us. Let's look at our focus for the profile of a godly woman. Sprinkled all through the Scriptures, we find direction and an example of what it is and what it isn't. We see where individuals succeeded and where individuals failed, and we need to remember that we learn from both. But I do feel drawn to one particular text: "Be ye holy, for I am holy" (1 Peter 1:16).

God is so purely direct in His challenges to us. He says this loud and clear. We are to recognize there is a certain image, a certain standard, a certain reputation He wants us to uphold because we belong to Him. Really, this verse speaks to all the elements of our foundation. So let's break it apart.

Holy—Holiness

What is your first reaction to the word *holiness*? Women in long skirts? A charismatic church? Maybe I am too blunt here. If I were honest, in my immature days—yes, even as a believer—those were my reactions. I had holiness in my mind as a practice of a church, instead of a purpose of a Christian. It goes beyond the demonstration of apparel and activity choice, but deeper into understanding who God is and who He desires us to be. Then I came to an understanding—"In all thy getting, get understanding" (Proverbs 4:7)—and I learned holiness is a standard, a way that my walk should be identified. It should be my operating procedure, my mission that I have chosen to accept. However best you look at it, consider this: It's our way of living. And what does it look like? It looks like God.

God calls us to be like Him, pure in nature and character. Sometimes that means being refined through fire, but it's a call toward victory as a result of that fire. Don't get scared by the smoke, but know whatever trial you find yourself in, God has you covered, and you will emerge whole.

And the charge says to *be* holy. It doesn't say to put it on when someone is looking or act holy or dress holy. It says to *be*, which means our dress, our conversation, and our interactions will result in holiness because it is an outpouring of what is on the inside, the identity of Christ. It is continuous, a way of life. Simply put, *be*.

And why should we be holy? Because He is holy. It is about being set apart and consecrated. It means being different. Consider that as your glowing permission slip to be your unique self. Be set apart, allowing your special gifts, personality, and style to shine for Him. We are a representative of God, which brings us right back to reputation. We are ambassadors for Christ and serve as representation for Him. We can't expect people to be drawn to Him if they don't know what He looks like.

Authenticity

Now let's hit the third key of authenticity. A solid reputation and character has to be something that is said of us, not occasionally or a passing compliment that is rare, but our true, consistent identity. When an artist does a work of art, they often use a "Certificate of Authenticity." It declares the integrity of the artist's work, demonstrating its worth, value, and distinction. The elements of a certificate of authenticity can include the name of the piece, the date it was created, the dimension, the details, and an official signature approving the standard of the work. This certificate not only acknowledges the artist but allows others who experience their work to recognize its authenticity.

This concept challenges me to think first. I must know my value and whether my reputation is one of distinction or a copycat of someone else's work. Do I know the intricate details about myself and my character, and am I proud to put that on display for others? Most importantly, can I sign off with confidence and assurance that my words and deeds appropriately characterize me?

Reputation

So, let's circle back to reputation. If you are upholding a standard of godliness consistently, your home is known for the light you maintain. While your husband is at the gate, you can best believe that those at the gate would speak of a brightly lit home.

TCB #5: Knowing My Reputation

Consider your personal certificate of authenticity. Can you articulate your unique features' consistency with God's design of you and put your sign of approval on it?

My **ASK**. "What specific question(s) do I need to ask God?"

God's **ANSWER**. "What do I hear God saying in response to my question?"

My **ASSIGNMENT**. "What do I do with what God said? What do I need to do differently? What bold move or courageous step do I need to take? What change of direction do I need to make?"

God's **ASSURANCE**. "What does God's Word say to me?"

_____

_____

_____

_____

_____

_____

_____

_____

_____

_____

_____

_____

_____

_____

_____

_____

CHAPTER 6

~~~~

MY REASONING

I like to ask questions. Okay, a lot of questions. Yes, my hubby would be proud and surprised that I would so openly admit it, mainly because I often try to put a positive spin on my insatiable desire for questions, and I simply call my style "beneficial curiosity."

He will chuckle to himself, and I don't know if it is his husband's wit coming out, or his pastoral humbling when he asks me, "Beneficial for who?"

And I have to take a second thought at the question and ask myself, *Who is getting value from the questions I am trying to answer?* That test alone makes me rethink my approach. And I have to do it often because I am hardwired for curiosity.

I am the existential probe master, if that is even something to be proud of. In fact, I don't dig for answers; I excavate. Somehow, this digging skill and curiosity came very early on as I was growing up. I was definitely my parents' most inquisitive child, and I can imagine my sister and brother sharing a loud amen to that. My family would find me asking questions at the top of their day, when they arrived home from a busy day, on vacations, long car rides, in the middle of the night, in the middle of a movie, and more. Any place or opportunity to stimulate my imagination would find my gears going, and I was always hungry to learn more. While my siblings were ever so patient with me, I think they also found entertainment in provoking my curiosity.

I remember when I was a small child, my older sister, who of course was the most intelligent person in the world in my mind, told me, "Sissie, did you know that if you head up midway on the hill in the backyard and dig, you can actually reach China?" Well, why did she tell that to a curious, determined child like me? Almost daily, I would get my tools, which of course my sister conveniently supplied me with, to head up the hill and tackle my backyard discovery challenge. With spades, kitchen spoons, and pans from the kitchen (yes, I was a self-appointed archaeologist at work!), I would head up to my dedicated plot at the top of the hill, where I set myself on an adventure. And I dug, and I dug, and I dug.

The challenge compelled me, the doubt from my older brother drove me to prove him wrong, and the red clay I came across (yes, I was digging deep), inspired me to reach the red flag somehow. Those daily excavations went on for quite some time as I would turn the other way when my mom would ask why her spoons were bending and her pans smelled like outside. My father finally intervened and rescued me from being the comedic relief as he maintained my self-esteem. He gently told me one day that I just might not reach this specific goal I had, but "Kid," as he would call me, "one day you can get to China, but not this way."

Let me tell you how much of a mark that made. If you were to visit my parents' house, you would see that grass still has yet to grow in the bald spot at the top of the yard, thanks to my crazy attempts. It became a running family joke and a proper place for me to explore my imagination. And spiritually, the mark was left on me of a lesson on determination. When balanced and exercised in wisdom, determination has its due place. But when exercised while ignoring wise counsel, absence of results, and selfish ambition (mine was to prove my brother wrong), you can be left with disappointment and destruction.

It sounds so harsh, but I am grateful for even the revelation and lesson God provides amid working on us no matter the time or the place. I remember sitting in an airport and feeling God's nudge of instruction during the wait for a delayed flight. And yes, of course, being me, I had a million questions at that time, wanting to understand the reason for the delay. But pulling out my laptop and typing feverishly away, lessons streamed in for me to grasp that the pause in my travel plans was simply a pause for me to sit still for a minute and listen. God needed to speak.

Back to the lesson on disappointment and destruction. I have learned that my relentless inquisition can be harmful. A spot that my parents wanted to be a plot of beauty and a place for things to grow, I destroyed with my digging. Despite the planting of seeds, the tireless watering, and hopeful waiting, my consistent digging never let the pause happen for the seed to root and for new life to grow. There are plots in our lives that God wants left alone and allowed to grow, that our disruption and relentless, personally driven actions can end up damaging for the long haul. In marriage, there are seasons of planting that the Lord performs. There's a time for Him to dig up ground so that it is prepared. There's a time for His seeds for future blessing to be established with the intention that we would do our job tending to it, watering the good seed, and expecting growth patiently instead of letting our desires get in the way by tearing up developing ground with our selfish digging.

Let me give you a practical example. I can recall several times when I had gone to God about something I wanted to see differently in my husband. My husband is an introvert, and I, on the other hand ... well, am not. He processes things internally, and I process out loud. While he works best through quietness, I work best through questions. Now admittedly, my approach of wanting to see a shift in my husband didn't start with prayers. I would constantly ask him, "Why don't you share with me? ... Why won't you tell me what's on your mind? ... Why won't you let me in?" His commitment to being quiet remained, and I shifted my focus.

I shifted to plan B, which should have been my plan A. When he didn't answer, then I took the questions to God. *Why doesn't he share with me? Why won't he tell me what's on his mind? Why won't he let me in?* And God convicted me and first showed me that the tone, timing, and tenacity in which I was asking was misaligned. My tone was one of indignation. I felt offended by my husband's silence and placed myself in a position of righteous anger that he had to tell me everything on his mind and tell me when I asked, expecting him to answer on my time. My timing was my own, inconsiderate of his space and time and what filled his mind. And my tenacity was, for me, justified because, hey, I am a determined woman who can get things accomplished, including getting her husband to talk. My displeasure in his silence had slowly slipped into anger. And this was not a healthy place for him, for me, or for our relationship.

I thank God He stepped in. He showed me how to change my tone, my timing, and my tenacity. I had to put the shovel down and stop digging. My husband needed to hear my spirit of genuine curiosity and not criticism. Was I seeking to understand my husband's heart? His weight? His concerns? Or was I just looking for surface answers, ignoring some challenges he may have been facing deep down? And my timing had to change. It was not ideal to question him as soon as he got off a problematic phone call or when he was trying to unwind after a challenging day—especially asking questions that interrupted his hearing from God.

God had been planting seeds in my husband's heart and spirit to open up more and find ways to let me in. Yet, instead of me watering that good seed, I was simply taking a shovel and digging, not allowing the good seed to grow. And my tenacity! I should take pride in my steadfastness when it's for the value of another. I should recognize the power of shifting. Instead of using my energy to pummel my husband with questions, I should place that energy into raising up my prayers to God on his behalf.

I learned that there is a fine line between asking questions and seeking to understand. Very close, but we can ask questions to satisfy ourselves, our pride, our curiosity, our ego, etc. But seeking to understand pleases God and others and ultimately comes back to benefit us. Seeking to understand means you may get an answer that can go beyond your surface question.

God wants us to know that all questions are not to be answered, and all answers may not be ours to possess at the time we are seeking them. There is a blessing to being diligent, but the drive should come with wisdom. If I press my husband for answers without wisdom, I could be digging a plot that will lead to barrenness instead of fruitfulness.

I know my questions are connected to how I process and reason. I subject myself to my own line of questioning because I challenge myself to be purposeful in my thoughts and actions.

But "Mary, Mary, quite contrary," how should my garden of thoughts grow?

"Let this mind be in you, in which was also in Christ Jesus" (Philippians 2:5). This state of thinking, where humility is the foundation and honoring God is the focus, is what God desires for us. Our actions, our speech, our responses are all a result of our thinking, our reasoning. If we process our thoughts with selfish ambition, looking to satisfy ourselves, we don't end up with fruitful results.

But I do have a deep well of curiosity that can sometimes be insatiable. Thank God for a patient husband who can offer answers or a subtle nod when I have exhausted my inquiry allowance.

Patience, trust, and confidence in God's consistency can help us slow our pace and still our restless minds. Otherwise, if we are honest, the garden of our mind can become weedy with questions and unnecessary inquiries, crushing the life out of the peaceful thoughts God would much rather see flourish. I know my brain can become quite busy and filled with thoughts that prevent me from taking the proper time to reason through things. And where does that leave me? It leaves me with a garden of poor decisions, commitments with unstable roots, and seeds of regret that do not allow other seeds to grow and flourish.

Let's continue to water our garden with more Word.

TCB #6: Knowing My Reasoning

Let's consider; what is at the root of your reasoning? Where should God uproot unhealthy weeds and plant new seeds?

My **ASK**. "What specific question(s) do I need to ask God?"

God's **ANSWER**. "What do I hear God saying in response to my question?"

My **ASSIGNMENT**. "What do I do with what God said? What do I need to do differently? What bold move or courageous step do I need to take? What change of direction do I need to make?"

God's **ASSURANCE**. "What does God's Word say to me?"

_____
_____
_____
_____
_____
_____
_____
_____
_____
_____
_____
_____
_____
_____
_____
_____

CHAPTER 7

~~~

MY REACTION

S ir Isaac Newton, legendary physicist and mathematician, is going to help us with our next lesson. Let's go back to physics class, and here is where I do want you to dig. Dig deep and turn on your school memories, thinking for a minute as we let some science facts illuminate our next order of business to attend to—our reactions.

Newton may be a surprising character to pop up in this devotional journey, but that matches him as he was an individual with a surprising story. Though he grew to be a legendary breakthrough scientist and man of discovery, he was born a sickly child, small in form and low in strength. But that early identity did not determine or define his ability. He was not expected to live beyond his day of birth, let alone birth discoveries of truth in science that would last and be learned far beyond his days. That alone has God's signature on it. To do the impossible, perform the unexpected, and demonstrate strength and change that has long-lasting impact.

Let us do a bit of our own discovery to understand and appreciate how our reactions can change history in our marriages. Newton and his work have a lot of rich background as he brought to common knowledge the foundational principles of modern physics. But let's take a deeper dive into just one of his laws of motion. The third law stated this: For every action, there is an equal and opposite reaction.

As I mentioned, I love taking notions and life observations and translating them into spiritual principles. I am fascinated and appreciate how the God of the universe, who made all, can use all to teach us in some of the most creative ways.

Here we have this physics principle which we need to unpack. The premise of Newton's Third Law of Motion instructs us that as we look at intersections of objects, a phenomenon occurs when the two objects come in contact with each other. When they are in motion, their intersection, or coming together, leads to contact that results in movement. In other words, two bodies upon contact with each other apply forces to each other that are equal in magnitude yet opposite in direction. That's a lot to digest yet holds simple truth. Impact happens upon impact. As godly women, it is our duty to choose what impact we want to make.

My aim is not to refute the principle at all but for us to make a connection with it. When we intersect and come in contact with our mate, particularly in an intersection of frustration or confusion or disagreement, does the action lead to a similar reaction? Take anger, for example. Do we give back what we get, or do we apply Newton's theory and do the opposite of what our flesh and self-desire want to do? Relationships cannot be lived out in a healthy manner when our motives are built around a tit-for-tat model. And if we stay in Newton's thinking, as a matter of being in motion, consider when we are "in motion" with our emotions. Intersections of emotions can be an awfully slippery slope of damage if we do not attend to them carefully. Do we feel compelled for our reaction to return in kind what was given to us, or do we shift our thinking and choose a different and more productive direction? There comes with this dynamic of opposite energy a more positive impact that can serve our marriages well.

Going back to Newton's law, take for example a bird flying. This is often used to understand the law of motion through an application in nature. When a bird flies, he flaps his wings and pushes air down. The bird receives a thrust of motion as a result of the intersection of the bird's wings and the air. The energy the bird places from within to push on the air encounters a reverse energy from that air pushing up, which actually pushes the bird up to soar. That grabs me! Let's put some Word on it. In Isaiah 40:30–31, God declares for us, "Even the youths shall faint and be weary, and the young men shall utterly fall; but those who wait on the Lord shall renew their strength. They shall mount up with wings like eagles; they shall run and not be weary; they shall walk and not faint." I know we will have mornings we are tired, afternoons when we grow weary, and evenings when feel like our energy is past empty, but do you see that how we handle our reactions can restore us and renew our strength and in turn the strength of our marriages?

It's time to look at this deeper. When we encounter an energy from our mate that may cause us to want to return that negative energy, let's switch it and provide an opposite positive reaction so that it gives us the push we need to move up and not away. To advance and not retreat. To soar and not falter. We must choose in every encounter with our mate whether we will respond either productively or destructively by the way we show up and offer ourselves in our reactions. It won't always be easy or come to mind right away, but that is why we take the time to take care of our business, develop skills, and use our tools for success in our relationships.

In the earlier days of my career, when I was working in corrections, I started there as an intern with an awesome mentor who remains a sage source of wisdom in my life. As part of my career development journey, I had aspirations and associated steps that would grow my skills and experience from working in our headquarters environment to moving into the field to be in amid the prisons we were tasked to serve. Working in the prison was a whole new dynamic that required a different level of skill and preparedness to operate and lead effectively. My mentor was a dedicated coach who fully believed in the power of immersion, which included frequent facility support visits where I began to learn the ropes working inside. As I got closer to the opportunity to shift to a full-time role working daily in the prison and not just intermittent visits, I was gearing up to understand all the requirements, expectations, and training provided to serve in such a capacity. I learned that team members in the institutions were taught a very specific set of skills for their personal safety and the safety of others around them. They were not assigned a weapon to carry as that could result in a tragedy if that weapon was turned on them and used against them, but they learned the martial art of aikido.

I was fascinated by the approach and the intentions of aikido. It's an age-old practice for self-defense, known as a way to "harmonize energy." It is an approach that depends upon the individual under attack not to return the same force from the attack, but to maintain calm, attention and focus, and physical self-control to subdue, but in no way is it exercised to create harm.

Imagine if we applied mental aikido in our relationships in the way we communicate and engage. One key aspect that stands out to me is the core principle of a master of aikido—being a master of self-control. It intrigues me as it is seen as a martial art of graceful refinement yet developed through rigorous training and discipline. I want that to be said of my character as a wife, that my combination of grit and grace is a result of being intentional to train and discipline my mind and heart so that my actions do not cause harm. This requires me to know my triggers and be self-aware of how I am impacting others, particularly my mate. I have to remind myself often that his place at the gate is not devoid of issue, challenge, and struggle, so why should he come home to another place of combat? My home should be a breath of fresh air and renewed energy for him and not a boxing ring of continued struggle.

A few years into my marriage, God brought me back to a lesson I have shared with other couples. In fact, my husband's godson drew it on his whiteboard as a reminder. It was a simple statement from my father: Fight the problem, not the person. What exactly do I mean by that, you may ask? Nearly 100 percent of the time, all problems have roots. I can't think of any issue, concern, or problem that has surfaced in my marriage that was a "just because" issue. Don't get me wrong, some roots can be deeper, run stronger, and have longer history. But things on the surface have meaning below. If we are not careful, the words that come out of our mouths and the actions we demonstrate will lead us incorrectly and unfruitfully to dealing with only what we see and hear in front of us. And what we see and hear is the person in front of us, and we end up singularly reacting to what we see versus getting to the heart of what we need to look for—the roots. We should look at what is the root of the issue and recognize roots that will require the strength of two sets of hands to pull up and out.

Hold on to these thoughts for consideration:

- Hurt people hurt people. Seek to understand the energy that is not positive when it comes from your husband. Is there a pain he is dealing with, and you may just be caught in the unfortunate crossfire of his issue? Pray for him, don't fight him.

- Recognize where the real issue is and fight the right fight. The battle is one against those things that try to come against your marriage. Your husband is not the enemy. The enemy is the issue. If you miss this, you will find yourself swinging your words like a prizefighter and run the risk of finding yourself, when the bell has rung, fighting to exhaustion, and instead of carrying on, you're ready to walk out.

- For every action there is an equal reaction—but what should it be? Is the reaction building up or tearing down? And this is not just in marriage but in any relationship. This is for all relationships, so we are putting our tools to work in broad ways. Consider the relationships you have and how your reactions have caused stress and made the relationship suffer. Those are the actions to avoid. Compare that to times when your actions led to healing because you shifted the way you reacted. Those are the actions to repeat.

Remember, it can be very small steps that create sizable change. Think of it as a rudder in a ship. If you want to change the course of the way your marriage sets sail, you can alter your reactions with even the words you speak. You can either find yourself in the storm and continue further into it or steer away from it and head to safety. When we find ourselves in a storm of emotions, the rudder of our tongue, if we are not careful with our words, can steer us further into a storm. But as wise women, if we choose the right reaction, our words can guide us out.

TCB #7: Knowing my Reactions

Let's consider our nature of how we react, especially in times of storms of emotions. Do we know our triggers, and are we self-aware of how our behavior impacts our marriage's ability to soar?

My **ASK**. "What specific question(s) do I need to ask God?"

God's **ANSWER**. "What do I hear God saying in response to my question?"

My **ASSIGNMENT**. "What do I do with what God said? What do I need to do differently? What bold move or courageous step do I need to take? What change of direction do I need to make?"

God's **ASSURANCE**. "What does God's Word say to me?"

_____

_____

_____

_____

CHAPTER 8

~~~

MY RESISTANCE

If we carry on our learning from understanding our reactions and knowing what our triggers are, there is a connection to how we react to things, where if we are not careful, it can turn into resistant behavior. We all know what that looks like. Our defenses go up, and our mind goes into what we may think is self-preservation mode but can be others' damaging mode. I'll use myself as an example. If I could introduce a new defensive sport to the Olympics, I would be a gold medalist "shut downer." What exactly is an Olympic shut downer? Well, so glad you asked. This sport requires a few skills, which include speed, muscle, and focused attention. The traits that aren't demonstrated are accuracy and any type of team building.

If you were to see the first round in an Olympic shut downer contest, you would witness the competitors' lightning-speed ability to quickly pull in all feelings, including their conversation and interaction with anyone, especially someone whom they have identified as an opposing team member. You would also see their muscle demonstrated in the developed skill that my grandmother would call hard-headedness, where they are fixed and focused on their own emotions and tuning out others. Finally, that leads us to the last combination skill set of focused attention and lack of team building as this is a recoiling into self and one-person sport. No interaction, no openness, and no engagement. I can even picture the commentators calling the moves on the sidelines.

Commentator 1: "There she goes. She has entered the ring of dialogue with her mate. Yes, folks, she served up her thought to him.

Commentator 2: "And there we have it. He didn't respond."

Commentator 1: "Well, from the looks of it, he offered a response and served it back, but I don't think it was what she was looking for. In fact, I see him leaning in and looking like he wants to inquire."

Commentator 2: "Yes! She is on her game! She withdrew. Moved back a few spaces on the couch. It's as if I can see her planning her next move. Her laptop is open. Wow, she did the silent you-just-don't-get-it move!"

Commentator 1: "Wait, I see her positioning herself ... feet up under her ... hand under her chin, looking straight ahead ... and yes, there we have it ... turning to the edge of the sofa now. It's interesting because she could just leave the room, but she stays there. I wonder what her next move will be. Staying and making us wait for it—that is a gold medal move right there."

Commentator: 2: "Oh, she grabbed another piece of equipment. Yes, the headphones! She has officially tuned out. And boy, is she typing away on her computer. I sure wish we could see what she was writing and even more what she is thinking."

Commentator 1: "Well, we will tune back in and see how this round plays out. By the look on her face, which isn't one of fire, it's just cool ice, this may be a while."

Yes, I admit, I have my fair share of gold medals in this sport and times that I am not proud of. We all can think of a "sport" we are not proud of. Perhaps you have medaled in the game of "deflection," calling out all blame except for the behaviors you own, or "issue inflation," allowing the problem to be bigger than it is. Whether we have gotten gold, silver, or bronze, we must not celebrate the habits tied to our emotions but pay attention to advancing our ways and shifting our sport to more godly and productive behaviors that will result in true wins in our marriages and homes.

God always flips learning for me. And as He convicted me on my own sport of "shut downer," He challenged me on my resistance, which admittedly hit me hard. I tried to rationalize to God that I shut down to reflect, and He pushed back to show me I shut down to resist. But He didn't leave me there. He took me back to a comment my son had made on a trip to Florida. After sharing with me that he needed some of Mom's home remedies for his stuffy nose, I told him my first prescription was going to be to advise him to get some rest to build up his resistance. When your body is fatigued, your resistance is down, and you are at risk for sickness.

God gave us these wonderfully intricate bodies with systems, organs, connections, and more, including our immune system—an internal operating system to keep us safe by being a defense against disease. It can detect what is good for you and what will harm you and not only detect but fight against what will cause harm, so you can be well. And it hit me, as I felt challenged, that all the energy I put into resisting things like apologies that come packaged differently than I imagined, or advice that my success is a result of purpose and not popularity, that I have to flip my mental model on resistance. Instead of *being* resistant, I need to *build* my resistance to ward off those things that will cause sickness in my marriage.

My sister-friend, that is our charge! We must keep our eyes open, our mind alert, and our right-behavior ready to fight off the viruses that will attack our marriage. Sounds odd, right? Well, let's explore what that looks like.

Viruses, bacteria, and germs are small and can live in a variety of environments, and when they get into our bodies, they wreak havoc if they are not treated. There are "viruses" of pride, "bacteria" of gossip, and "germs" of greed that all will lead to harm. They can start small and almost undetected if we are not careful. There are germs that enter our minds and hearts, manifest in our homes, and lead to sickness in our marriages. We can wake up one day and wonder, *What happened to the strength of our relationship? Where did the vitality go in our connection? Why does my heart not beat the same?* It may be because we didn't fight off what has now crept in and is causing illness in our marriage.

But the good news is, God is a healer—mentally, physically, emotionally, spiritually, and more. But remember, when He gifts us with healing, we have to do our job at maintaining the wellness, and I do believe it is through keeping up our resistance. Just like building up your physical resistance to fight off sickness through a healthy lifestyle, your relational resistance is built up the same way.

My younger sister is a certified personal trainer and nutrition coach. She is personally committed to healthy living and helping others on the same journey for discovering and experiencing wellness. One thing I love about her work is when she engages a client, she listens before advising so that there is a flexible plan that can be sustainable. She maps out a solid training plan for nutrition and exercise based on the client's desires. I will follow her model and suggest a healthy marriage plan for us to build up our resistance. Let's consider a few factors that will help us physically and relationally.

- What do you consume—do you eat the fruit of joy, peace, patience, kindness, goodness, faithfulness, gentleness, and self-control (Galatians 5:22–23)?
- How much sleep do you get? A healthy marriage also has a component of intimate activity, which, yes, can take sleep away. But that is allowed! On the serious side, does your marriage get the rest it needs from distractions, other responsibilities, and other individuals who consume your time (Mark 6:31)?
- What level of activity is in your relationship? Is it idle or thriving? Are the memories of special times and adventures and new explorations few and far between? Get your marriage in regular motion, active and vibrant (Proverbs 15:19–21).
- What are you exposed to? Do you breathe in the pollution of pessimistic thinking or the fresh air of God's hope (Job 33:4)?

- Are you maintaining a healthy weight? Are you carrying unforgiveness, guilt, shame, unspoken desires, and anxieties? That can be unhealthy pounds of burden that will cause your marriage to move slowly and unproductively. Those things need to be shed and can be worked off through good communication, prayer, and commitment (Hebrews 12:1).
- Do you have good marriage hygiene? Do clean thoughts fill your mind as it relates to your partner? Do you avoid bringing in dirt of gossip, malice, and contention into your home (Philippians 4:8)?
- What is the stress level in your home? Is your home a place of peace? Is your communication engaging to allow your partner to release (James 3:18)?

These are just a few tips that can help us build up our resistance to fight the bad that will come against the good in our marriage. Let's strive for health-filled marriages that have a longer life expectancy with remarkable joy.

TCB #8: Knowing my Resistance

My **ASK**. "What specific question(s) do I need to ask God?"

God's **ANSWER**. "What do I hear God saying in response to my question?"

My **ASSIGNMENT**. "What do I do with what God said? What do I need to do differently? What bold move or courageous step do I need to take? What change of direction do I need to make?"

God's **ASSURANCE**. "What does God's Word say to me?"

_____

_____

_____

_____

_____

_____

_____

_____

_____

_____

_____

_____

_____

_____

_____

_____

_____

_____

_____

_____

CHAPTER 9

~~~

MY REFLECTIONS

My mind goes back to another trip I had taken back home to Maryland. I was on a mission for a surprise visit to honor my mentor, Vanessa, at her retirement celebration. It was such an enjoyable, Spirit-filled event, and without fail, every time I am in her presence, I get energized and refueled. There is always some lesson I can glean from her or from being around her. I had found myself at five thirty the following morning after the event sitting in the airport reflecting on the evening I had just experienced. I had gone to celebrate the culmination of her rich career journey, which was full of challenges and overcoming. Vanessa was presented with honors, and memories were shared about the legacy she left throughout the progressions in her career. As people showered her with gifts, well wishes, war stories, and roasts, I sat back and realized it was a gift for me to have been a part of her life and a beneficiary of her influence.

Though I surprised her with my visit, I was honored when the individuals who organized the event recognized me and approached me. They knew I was one of her mentees and had grown a lot under her leadership and even after I had left the organization. They offered me the opportunity to speak, and though it was impromptu, I told them it would be an honor, not to mention one thing Vanessa always taught me was to be ready. So with delight I started to put my mind around the words I could share with others about how she impacted my life and modeled godly leadership and many other attributes that continue to be a sound investment to me. It was an easy gathering of thoughts as I reflected on all the opportunities she gave me, the wisdom she poured into me, the guidance, support, challenge, and more.

That was all the positive business around reflections from that evening. But let me give you a peek into where God had to develop me.

Selfishly, the evening was a time of memories for me. God had allowed me to build relationships with several individuals during my ten-year tenure with such a great organization, which was a pivotal milestone in my career on the East Coast. Having moved away to the Midwest, I had not seen many of these former colleagues for more than five years, and it was so special to reconnect. I moved around the room, greeting and laughing and reminiscing. I moved around that room like I had never done before. I walked through with a new style, a new success story, and a new shape! I had gone through a weight-loss journey, and it was like going back to a school reunion ready to show off.

As I moved about in my reconnecting, I shared updates of my life—my God-fearing hubby, my amazing son, my loving family, my growing church, the work in my career, which was flourishing, and community involvement. I sashayed through the crowd and shared stories about my new global job and the countries I had visited, the leaders I was working with, the new boards I was invited to serve on, and more. Admittedly I was more concerned with how I looked and wanted them to notice the physical change I worked so hard on. But then I noticed how many people told me, "You look so happy! ... This guy makes you light up. ... Marriage looks good on you." And to each response, I had to smile, and on the inside smile even harder and admit, *I am, he does, and it is.*

As I mentioned, I had developed relationships with these leaders, and they had gotten to know me personally. They knew my singleness and the stories that went along with that. They knew how I was prayerful about the right man God would give to me. As I had been blessed with godly leaders to work with, many had even prayed with and for me as they saw me progress in my career, reminding me of my worth that one day God would have my Mr. Right for me. A few knew about John and would ask at times, "Who is this guy? ... Why is he taking you away from us? ... Have you ever even been to the Midwest?" As leaders who cared about me, they kept their eyes on me, and at this time of reuniting, they definitely had their eyes on me and saw more than I expected.

People who see you day in and day out don't always catch incremental change. It's like losing weight, a few pounds here and there, and you get excited, but you feel like you can't totally see the results that others may see. But time and distance can make the difference and somehow can magnify the difference in you that others see. In my mind at this work reunion, I had been successful in a weight-loss journey, and I admit, I was thinking, *I am going to surprise a few folks, and hey, catch a few compliments.* But as I look back, it was so much more valuable that they saw the reflection of the joy God had given me in the life I was blessed to have. And a huge part of that difference was my marriage. That reflection of joy was more apparent, more glaring, than the vain desire for attention on my weight loss. They were just as proud of me in my marriage as they were in my professional development, if not more.

These were leaders who ran prisons, leaders with the skill and art of suspending judgment on people and seeing them for who they are, leaders whose eyes could look with meaning and see meaning in individuals. You couldn't get much past them. It was the nature of their work and the gift that they had, a different kind of eye. When encountering me, that same eye saw the difference. As I shared stories about my husband, which came easy, I was able to help them learn more about who he was and specifically who he was to me as I reflected him, and he wasn't even in the room. The impact he had on my life was apparent.

Proverbs 31:30 comes to mind. "Charm is deceitful, and beauty is passing, but a woman that fears the Lord, she shall be praised." Now what does that have to do with marriage? A woman who fears God, is in awe of Him, recognizes His sovereignty, and strives to submit to His will and control is a woman who wanted to obey in her singleness. I waited for Him to move, knew He would bring me to my Boaz, and am now living God's will for my life in the ministry of marriage. People who compliment me are not praising me but praising the God *in* me, and it only happens when I reflect Him.

My husband made me smile just thinking about him and reflecting on who he is for and to me. It shows in how I reflect that joy about the man I am married to. Some days we all have to admit it's hard because joy may not be top of mind, but do you have the treasures in the well of your heart, mind, and soul to draw from so the reflection can come out? It's the same way God desires us, the church, to be married to Him. (Ephesians 5:21–32). People should look at us and see God. They should be able to say, *Being a King's kid looks good on you.* We should reflect God's love and share our story about how He stays with us through the challenges and helps us to overcome, the joy He provides, and the continuing care of our heart. When they see us, they should see Him.

As a kid, did you ever try to take a mirror and put it in the sunshine and flash the light? You could catch someone, or even yourself, and the light could be so intense it could be blinding. At the right angle, a mirror in the presence of light will take the light and reflect that light, that energy, in another direction. Ultimately, we should always position ourselves first to catch the light of God, and at the right angle, we can effectively reflect His light and energy into the presence of others.

God has placed light in us. We come with that, and remember, your light drew your husband to you. He is not the source, just a part of how God illuminates your light, enhancing its brightness.

TCB #9: Knowing My Reflections

This book has been a journey, and my hope is that you have had some transforming experiences as we are moving along. Can you reflect on what that has been for you so far? Does it show and reflect the growing love with and for your husband and the investing love from God?

My **ASK**. "What specific question(s) do I need to ask God?"

God's **ANSWER**. "What do I hear God saying in response to my question?"

My **ASSIGNMENT.** "What do I do with what God said? What do I need to do differently? What bold move or courageous step do I need to take? What change of direction do I need to make?"

God's **ASSURANCE**. "What does God's Word say to me?"

_____

_____

_____

_____

_____

_____

_____

_____

_____

_____

_____

_____

_____

_____

_____

_____

_____

_____

CHAPTER 10

~~~

MY RIGHTS

Yes, *Erickajoy. I know you have been talking about all the things I must do and be committed to and the expectations set forth for me in my role as a wife. I recognize the challenge I have with this role God has entrusted me with, by being married or desiring to marry a man of stature. But now, I am glad you got to me, and you finally are going to address what I get out of this deal.*

Well, sorry, not exactly. As godly women recognizing the fine position God has placed us in to even have a hubby at the gate, we must remain mindful of the fact that, even if you are the ultimate diva, it's not about you. Yes, I hate to break it to you, but I do recall the diva-shattering moment in my life when that hit me so that I will be compassionate.

My fortieth birthday had arrived, and though my husband is not one for surprises himself, he knows how much I love them. He had a whole week full of events set up for me. It started with a hosted lunch where he brought together women in my network, who were actually "gate girls" themselves, for a time of laughter, stories, reconnecting, and building new relationships. In the middle, he had a local hat maker design a wide brim pink hat for me that was absolutely stunning. And this gift was apropos as a hint for the weekend getaway to the Kentucky

Derby. He had listened to my dreams years before and made arrangements behind my back to bring a smile to my face. To top it all off, he had a logo created for me with my initials. At the close of my birthday, I noticed that this beautiful backdrop had an image that contained aspects of all my fortieth birthday surprises. He really went over the top to make it special, distinct, and memorable. I share all that to hopefully get you to join me as I rationalize out my diva moment that was shattered.

This culmination trip to the Kentucky Derby was magical. It was a dream on my bucket list, not so much for the actual horse race but the energy, ambience, and fun-filled weekend of activities that made the derby the draw that it is. Before we left, he had me pack for a weekend getaway with items bought on the shopping trip he had planned for the preparation. Night one, he had me at a purple-carpet gala with live painters, ice sculptures. We enjoyed a concert and comedy show front row with television stars on stage and retired athletes behind me. The next day, I got to don my custom hat, new dress, and heels and head to the derby with all the lovely fanfare awaiting me.

I wasn't selfish with my birthday trip, so I quickly secured some sharp outfits for my husband and son, who was six years old at the time. They had matching seersucker suits and, of course, fedoras along with white bucks—because in my mind, we were going to be picture perfect. I mean, hey, it was my birthday, but my record of it required all of us to look our best. Stick with me, and you'll understand the setup.

We were walking around the derby, trying to soak in all the excitement, energy, and effervescent classiness that comes with this annual get-together for the snazzy, where Churchill Downs creates an experience to remember. The crowd, the special time with my family, and the thought of one of my travel dreams come alive all filled me with excitement. My sassy came out even stronger as I looked around and saw the sea of Kentucky Derby hats and knew I could hold my own with my custom design and coordinated dress. It did no good for the passerby compliments, nods, remarks, and requests on where in the world I secured such a hat. Still with me?

So, this personalized logo, this weekend full of Erickajoy, attention, adventures, and all this celebration of me is running in my head—under this custom-made hat, mind you. And I see a reporter in the distance, interviewing attendees. She was donning a beautiful hat herself, and she started walking in our direction. I got out my phone and looked up the station based on the sticker I saw on the cameraman's vest. I believe in being prepared, so I was doing my homework to be ready to be showcased on the news. What birthday girl would miss an opportunity like this? What a way to put a cap on *my* special weekend! This lead news anchor came close to my family, and as I was straightening my dress and grabbing my lip gloss, she squatted down and started to interview my son! My six-year-old son. My "not me" son. And, yes, my husband and his witty, sarcastic self had this sheepish grin on his face that said to me, *You thought she was coming to interview you, huh?*

I could only shake my head, and it hit me. It's not about me. I had to get myself together quickly so I didn't mess up a special moment for my son. His outfit and fedora drew her, and his old soul and charm kept her. He is a brilliant child who surprises people, and he held his own. The interview was quite exciting and enjoyable, I must admit. As if it wasn't enough of a lesson, it was memorialized not only on the news that night, but also on the day news in the weeks following with pictures of this amazing kid at the Kentucky Derby in the paper. Talk about a diva-shattering moment.

So, let's get through this together. I want you to hold up your left index finger and point it to the sky. That symbolizes you. Next, take your right index finger and circle it a few times around that finger you extended, and say to yourself, "It's all about me … it's all about me … it's all about me."

Okay, good, we did it! We collectively had our moment of admission! Hopefully, it's out of your system. Now let's overcome that and wash your hands and your mind of that thought. Take those same hands and celebrate God working through you! He is your number one.

News alert: The world doesn't revolve around us. Admittedly it can feel like it, though, right? Many depend on us. In our homes, we are often the thermostat, setting the temperature and affecting the temperament of our husbands and children. At work, we are negotiators, decision-makers, counselors, strategists, and more, making improvements and solving problems. In the community, we are serving and leading at the same time, impacting lives and making change happen. All of this is true, but God is the reason why we are even in those positions and circumstances, He is the source for our energy, ability, and innovation to come alive and to make amazing all the business we take care of. So as women of God, we should be ever so careful and always on the lookout for the times when we creep back on the type of mindset of it being "all about me." If you ever feel that finger raise, catch yourself and remind yourself of the right perspective and call out God being number one.

Now that we had that moment, I am going to keep my word. We are going to look at our rights. Yes, we do have some.

We used our old science-class muscle, now let's go back for a history lesson to set the stage for this one. The founding fathers of our country made a strong statement about our rights as citizens of this country. Everyone has the absolute right to three offerings that should never be inhibited by anyone or anything. These are the right to life, liberty, and the pursuit of happiness, so stated—our inalienable rights.

As citizens of the kingdom of God, queens and princesses to be exact, we have the same rights and, honestly, an obligation to expect those rights in our home and marriage. Let's review our rights.

Life

This one is heavy because we know that life is what our Savior is all about. It's not just the everlasting life that He has provided to us as a condition of His will but also the life that is "more abundant" in this present time!

God once challenged me, in a previous relationship, about how I was wrestling with what I was experiencing in the relationship versus what I was expecting. I was very particular in my waiting for my mate, not picky, but particular because I held on to the understanding that I had to know my own worth as I considered the individual who would receive my time and attention. When we were together, I felt that I was missing something, which was hard for me to understand. He was a godly man who had a solid job and some great aspirations, yet I was still looking for more. The bad thing is, I couldn't explain the *more* and was not sure what was supposed to fill in that blank that I was feeling. I ended up feeling concerned that I was judgmental, unappreciative, and shallow. That was until the Holy Spirit spoke so sweetly, "Life more abundantly ... that your joy may be full."

> The thief does not come except to steal, and to kill, and to destroy: I have come that they might have life, and that they may have [it] more abundantly. (John 10:10)

> These things have I spoken to you, that My joy may remain in you, and that your joy may be made full. (John 15:11)

> Now may the God of hope fill you with all joy and peace in believing, that you may abound in hope, in the power of the Holy Spirit. (Romans 15:13)

At first, I was not getting the lesson as it related to relationships. I thought those verses were only to provide us guidance on our salvation. The Holy Spirit reminded me that a solid Christian does not compartmentalize their life. There are no borders that God sets up where He puts restraint or exclusions on His promises, so even in a relationship, God seeks to apply His power of abundance and looks to provide us with a joy that is full, and full means just that. The meaning of full doesn't include limitations. And it hit me, why would it not be that way? The ministry of marriage must resemble the relationship of Christ and His bride, which means, we have this right.

If you desire a relationship, don't settle. Don't pursue perfection but do have standards, and don't move into anything that places you beneath your opportunities.

This right and others must be exercised with godly caution and spiritual direction to avoid crashing and burning in arrogance and entitlement. If you are in a relationship where you are not experiencing joy, it's not your ticket to get out of the relationship, but it is an invitation to get out of the rut. Take the time to see what is causing the lack of joy, what is blocking the pipeline for it to reach you, and what steps you can take to rediscover the joy.

That is what I did. Because that precious word from the Holy Spirit left me in a place with more questions, I continued to ask them. Answers came that caused me to change direction, so I moved from that relationship and sought God's guidance. I was determined not to carry regret or remorse, and I allowed my Father to fill in the missing blank. In His sovereign way, that was His plan all along. There was a name He had in mind that would fill in that blank—John, His beloved, and now mine.

Every day with my husband is not sunshine, but when it's cloudy, we weather the storm together. "Go out of the ark, you, and your wife, and your sons, and your son's wives with you" (Genesis 8:16).

Liberty

Next, we get to liberty. This one must have the right angle as well. I know all of us can think of times where we feel like Lady Liberty. At the close of Emma Lazarus's Petrarchan sonnet, "The

New Colossus," she pens words as the voice of the Statue of Liberty that could perhaps feel like the weight we carry.

> Give me your tired, your poor,
> Your huddled masses yearning to breathe free,
> The wretched refuse of your teeming shore.
> Send these, the homeless, tempest-tost to me,
> I lift my lamp beside the golden door!

There are times I feel like I am carrying the weight of the masses, those in most need, those who are tired, and I am using my last ounce of strength to carry them. Those needs get sent to me, and I am tasked with being a light. All this is true and more. But the power of the Statue of Liberty's meaning is seen as we understand our history lesson. The statue was given as a gift of friendship from France to the United States of America as a reminder of the mutual desire for freedom. The statue has since become known as a beacon reminder of freedom, hope, and strength. That is also the gift the Lord gives us.

God wants to remind us that He makes the call and the offering for us to come to Him. He is the beacon that draws us in from the storm, raging waters, places of oppression, scenarios of slavery and grants new freedom for us to access. It is as if Emma channeled the Scripture that says, "Come unto me, all ye that labour and are heavy laden" (Matthew 11:28, emphasis added). God wants us to not only have liberty after we close our eyes from this life but as we are living *in* this life. He wants us to be able to let go of weights we carry.

Though what probably sticks most in our visualization of the Statue of Liberty includes what's in her hands and on her head, I feel one of the most inspirational elements of the figure is what is at her feet—broken chains.

That is the distinction of freedom, of true liberty: when what was once holding you bound, restricting your movement, limiting your capability, is shattered, and you are free. That is my prayer for you even in this moment. You have a right to and a resource for liberty. And you can absolutely seek God for that freedom. He holds many keys, and one key labeled *freedom* is yours for the asking. Call out the chains that are restricting you. Is it unforgiveness, shame, guilt, an unresolved issue with someone? Have you placed chains of self-doubt, fear, or apprehension on yourself?

Start at the base and look up. Start with the breaking of those chains; then your feet are free to move about. And your back will be stronger, you can stand taller, you can hold the word in your hands close to your heart, you can hold up the light that He gives you, and you can wear the crown of a woman who has handled her business. Wear it well and wear it freely.

Pursuit of Happiness

Last, the pursuit of happiness. The movie, *The Pursuit of Happyness*, may come to mind as you think of this phrase. It is the story of a man's journey of determination and relentless sacrifice for him and his son that took him from homelessness to a gate. His pursuit was very focused as he overcame challenge after challenge, including a broken marriage. But something within him continued to drive him and fuel him to reach his goals. *Happyness*, as the movie is labeled, was about what *he* saw as important. The Y was intentionally used to spell the word as a reminder of the *you* in happiness. I see it as looking at happiness in a tailor-made way. I believe happiness can be fleeting, and joy is sustained, but let's take a moment and focus on the pursuit.

Two key elements I want to call to mind that I believe the movie provides a valuable lesson on are priorities and perspective. We should anchor our pursuit in the right priorities. In the film, his main priority was his son. This helps us understand the Y, the focus of our *you*, this tailor-made pursuit. It's not us slipping back into thinking it is all about us, but it calls our attention to what is most important around us. Who is most important, and who are we called to serve?

This can change or evolve or shift as we grow in different seasons. Whether taking care of your children or then being a caregiver for an aging parent, your team at work, or your board you serve on, make sure God places the stamp of approval on your priorities. Trust me, He has had to convict me a few times because I am wired to troubleshoot, lead, and serve. But all the places I feel I should be are not always the prioritized places He wants me to go. Priorities should be short in number and laser focused. They should have a clearly articulated "why" and a meaningful understanding of your role.

The second element is perspective. Having the right perspective in life is critical. Perspective is a term used in art to help two-dimensional features come alive. An artist uses perspective to add distance and provide depth to their work to make it more exciting and realistic. The ability to manipulate lines directed to a vanishing point ends up creating distance that provides this depth to the work of art. Spiritually, that is what I believe we are called to do in our faith. The work of art is based on the artist's point of view, and this vanishing point is the central focus to create the work. I love the fact that it's called a vanishing point, because when I put God first and in the center of any situation, my doubts, fears, apprehensions, and concerns can vanish. They don't become the block to my work, and He refocuses my attention where it should be. Point of view and the vanishing point aid the artist in completing their work and completing it well.

I have gotten the chance to get to know Chris Gardner, whose life was the model for the movie (I talked to him, and not only did he grant me permission to mention him in the book, but he is super excited and said my book is timely). One thing I have appreciated in Chris when we would talk about the film was his transparency. He became an open book for others to get inspired, but he was transparent with himself in his progress in the pursuit and after. And his life was a story.

Guess what? You have a story as well. You have a pursuit God has called you to; are you ready for the work it takes to make it to where God has destined you to go? You are, I am certain of it because we didn't make it this far in our learning journey together for it to be any other way.

Hold on in knowing these are your rights—if you choose to exercise them. Exercise them with responsibility, and you will experience a great return.

TCB #10: Knowing my Rights

Shifting our thinking of rights is necessary as we grow from a mindset of entitlement to empowerment. God desires for us to have the latter and wipe out the former. In your time now for personal reflection, you can take all or just one of the rights and explore how it applies in your life for this season.

My **ASK**. "What specific question(s) do I need to ask God?"

God's **ANSWER**. "What do I hear God saying in response to my question?"

My **ASSIGNMENT**. "What do I do with what God said? What do I need to do differently? What bold move or courageous step do I need to take? What change of direction do I need to make?"

God's **ASSURANCE**. "What does God's Word say to me?"

_____

_____

_____

_____

_____

_____

_____

_____

_____

_____

_____

_____

_____

_____

CHAPTER 11

∿

MY REST

If you are a wife, mother, professional, community worker, or just about any female in today's world, you probably read the title and said, *Rest? What is that?* It reminds me of a conversation I recently had with a colleague on work-life balance; we emphatically agreed, that's a misnomer. First, because if you do work, it's just part of your life, and all the programs and support mechanisms in a company can't give you balance. That alone is up to you as an individual.

So am I going back on my word of empathizing with you and ensuring we make this contemporary woman a reality? Absolutely not. I just believe it's important to go in with eyes wide open. If we consider the type of woman whose husband is at the gate, let's make this assumption: That type of man did not marry a slacker. It's safe to say that she is one who has several responsibilities herself. In fact, that's what she is all about—taking care of business. But if we are honest, we know that business wears us out. It takes a toll on us physically, mentally, and spiritually. It's wear-and-tear for the journey. The blessing for us is that God has this tremendous warranty plan for us, as His special make and model, so that any repairs needed are covered, and He has a master technician to ensure they are done.

Isn't that comforting? When thinking back to when I was in college and I purchased my first vehicle on my own, my dad allowed—no, let's be honest here, required me to handle the transaction on my own. What I thought was cruel and unusual punishment was my father trusting that I had it in me, challenging me to stretch myself, and believing in me that I would come out successful in the end. Sounds like another Father I know.

Dad's belief in me was fuel to a belief in myself. It is something how others can water you with love and challenge and encouragement so that it extinguishes any flames of self-destructing doubt. So, I was careful and diligent in preparation for buying a car. I approached the opportunity with confidence. When looking at potential models, I remembered not to get too awed by the colors and the aesthetics, did the proverbial hood-opening to appear somewhat savvy. After a few trips to the dealership, I sat down in the office to sign papers for my first car.

Now when I purchased the car, I made certain to secure a warranty. I had done my homework, received coaching from Dad, and knew it was critical to get coverage for any unplanned trouble. Like insurance, I didn't plan or desire to have trouble, but if and when it came, I didn't want to wish I had planned. Yes, read that again.

I knew I needed some sort of plan to cover me. The dealer informed me that there was a basic warranty, which was good news, and an option for extended warranty for additional coverage. I had options, and I went for both.

This reminds me of our Spiritual Father. When God offers us the gift of salvation, He advises us of the warranty we have readily available. Just as when I pulled off the lot, I was covered, so when you leave the altar or stand from the side of the bed where you cried your heart out to receive Him, whatever awakening moment you have at the point of receiving Christ, you have a warranty. It is the great gift He gives unto us.

But we are mindful that there may be some trouble we face down the road that isn't your basic kind of damage, and we need to secure some sort of extended warranty. What does that look like? Prayer and fasting. The Word tells us how some things only go out by prayer and fasting. That's your extended warranty. But the wonderful thing is, the only cost to us is reaching out to the Lord.

So back to my first car. I remember when I first had to make use of my warranty. There was a repair that needed my attention yet someone else's skills. The brakes were screeching in my car at a level that became quite irritating, irritating enough that it grabbed my attention along with anyone who was in the local vicinity. The initial sounds were not too bad, and it came and went, but it was still a signal. Then individuals around me, like friends who would ride with me, even passersby, made comments that I had to really pay attention to. Until one day my brother carefully yet directly advised me, "If you don't take care of that, who knows what will happen. That could be a matter of life or death."

I had not taken it so seriously. I knew the warning signs, heard the cues, but was putting things off, unnecessarily so. Because remember, I had a warranty. I had coverage to take care of the issue. I didn't have the skills and expertise to take care of it, but I had access to someone who did.

All this may be starting to hit you. And I know I have asked you before, but stick with me here, as we get to the rest.

See, the car was giving me cues. This car was something I depended on every day for all I needed to do, which, even as a college student, was quite a lot. I would leave my apartment before six a.m. to drive about forty-five minutes to work, and then after a four-to-six-hour workday return to school to take afternoon and evening classes. Then, I wasn't finished. I would drive to my third-shift job at a credit card company. So, I needed my vehicle, but why wasn't I taking care of it? I depended heavily on it, but why didn't it have my full attention? Could we ask the same about ourselves—our bodies, hearts, and minds that we, along with our families and most of all the Lord, need? And we don't always attend to it.

Let's take the natural to spiritual. The car is us. There are people all around you, depending on you, whether it's literally driving your little one to tae kwon do classes or driving a young person toward a challenge as you mentor them, but *not* driving your spouse crazy. Let's take that driving off our lists. You have been created for someone. Someone needs you. We have to take note of the times we need attention. We ought to make time when we need the rest.

My car was giving me cues, very blatant cues. Trust me, even people on bus stops would give me the look as though I was deaf. But I ignored them—the cues and the bystanders. I still ask God, *Was it stubbornness? Laziness? Independence?* I am not certain still, but I do know it was not the right choice, particularly so because I had options. If you recall, I had a warranty on my car—a coverage set up so that if something like this did arise, I could at least inquire to see if I was covered.

And so yes, I finally did. It dawned on me that I had a problem, but I didn't have the skills it takes to fix it. And the lingering thought that it could be a matter of life or death began to trouble me. Whether that life was my own, or one unknown, I would still be negligent. Something had to change.

The special make and model that God crafted us to be, though designed for the long haul, is prone to break down if we don't take special care of this special model. It's because we are flesh. But remember, though we are made of flesh we are not constrained by flesh. The limitations that come with being flesh are not the extent of our experience when you tap into the "Flesh Maker." See, my car on its own couldn't fix itself, let alone assess itself to see what the issue was. But I had to take it to the dealer, who knew the ins and outs, and who could analyze the situation and present a solution.

You may be hearing the cues in your life from others around, maybe even from those you don't know, who see or hear that something is wrong. Don't try to figure it out or fix it, just take it to the model maker. But remember, that means you have to relinquish control, and there may be some space and time that changes your plans. If I go back to the car, I knew I wouldn't have access to my car for some time, but I had to hand it over to be taken care of, fixed, and ready to be back on the road.

That's the type of rest God desires for us. When we get to where we are seeing, hearing, and feeling the cues, we need to pull over and get some help. Yes, we were designed to be an ever-running engine, but we also received wisdom to attend to the cues. For when my car had its "rest" in the garage, there was no one trying to run across town in it, no one trying to borrow it, no one trying to get to the next place, but it was tucked away in a dedicated spot with a team of skilled hands to fix what wasn't operating the way it was designed to operate.

My cousin couldn't drive it, my roommate couldn't borrow it, I couldn't get use of it, but it was in capable hands rather than reckless hands. And those capable hands did what they do so well; they fixed my brakes and got me back on the road.

Back to our question about whether we know what rest is. We know it's needed. We know God can handle it and us in it. But ignoring the need for rest is detrimental for the journey. And it could be a matter of life or death. Why don't we get it?

Consider what is taking up time in your schedule. Not that those activities are bad. I truly believe everything that seems good isn't God's good for you. Think of this: How many candy drives, car washes, potluck dinners, book club gatherings, tutoring clinics, mentor sessions, board meetings, neighborhood cleanups, and soccer games can one person attend to? Not to mention the number of lemonade stands, firehouse drives, clothing donation receptacles, and car washes you passed along the way. How much can one person do? How much should one person do? They are good things, but are they God's choices for you?

I was once working on an online tool that I used at my job. You can log in and create interview guides when hiring a potential new hire. To generate the guide you had to click on a button that said "Select" to identify the areas you wanted to include in your interview guide. And for the super interviewer, there was a special button that said "Select All." I thought I would be that superwoman of an interviewer and proudly hit "Select All." What I got as an output overwhelmed me and pulled the wind from the superhero cape that was blowing off my back. The cape went flat, and so did my face when I realized I had chosen too much. There was a whole novel of interview questions. I imagined a candidate getting glassy-eyed in front of me, saw myself getting absolutely worn out, and saw the interview go downhill. Why did I select all? Why did I try to take on too much? They were all good questions, but not all needed.

I looked at the screen as if it could save me out of this one, and graciously it did. The screen offered to return me to the Home menu. And let me tell you, sometimes there is no place like home. I went back to the beginning with a fresh perspective, a more realistic goal, and started again. I looked at the list, and there was a phrase right below that I caught this time. First I noticed that when I went back in, it was still on Select All and all the areas were included by default. But that phrase that I mentioned that caught my eye simply said "Deselect All." I could have a fresh start! I didn't have to go with what was imposed on me. I didn't need to be unnecessarily overwhelmed. I could start fresh, make some solid decisions, and come out with a manageable solution and product that fit my needs and would still yield good results.

How many of us are walking around carrying the loads and weight of Select All? How many times have we stepped into a role, a responsibility, and taken on the default—taken on someone else's expectations—feeling committed and bound to someone outside of us and the Lord? Independently, each choice is noble and rewarding, but collectively, they are overwhelming and laborious to the point of exhaustion and no enjoyment. I learned a great lesson that day that has stuck with me, and I challenge you to let this be a sticking point: There is power in deselecting.

Let me go a little farther. There is power, liberty, freedom, the release of anxiety, and emancipation all in deselecting! We must carefully choose and confirm with God those things we take on. And the things that don't belong, deselect. He desires a life of liberty for us, and He is bothered as much if not more when we are unnecessarily burdened.

So back to the question of how do I get my rest. There is something right now that could possibly be taking its place. Seek God to find out what is in the way of your rest, rest of your body, rest of your mind and spirit.

TCB #11: Knowing My Rest

I want you to take some dedicated time and prayerfully seek God on why you picked up this book and what you want to get out of this journey.

My **ASK**. "What specific question(s) do I need to ask God?"

God's **ANSWER**. "What do I hear God saying in response to my question?"

My **ASSIGNMENT**. "What do I do with what God said? What do I need to do differently? What bold move or courageous step do I need to take? What change of direction do I need to make?"

God's **ASSURANCE.** "What does God's Word say to me?"

_____

_____

_____

_____

_____

~~~

UNTIL WE MEET AGAIN

Who is the "we"? It is us; it is you and God; it is you and your accountability partner; it is you and your mate. I aimed to offer as much as I could from my lived experience for a shared journey toward the business we have to take care of as we find ourselves in the blessing of being married to the amazing men we have in our lives. I want to leave you with a few thoughts as we come to the close of reading of the book. It is not an end, but a close of this first pass at building our plan, using all the tools laid out. We took the time to learn, laugh, and lean in on new discoveries and then made a personally committed challenge to seek God's guidance on the things we need to attend to and change. And we received assurance that no matter the circumstance, there are promises in His word that will carry us.

All that you've read is about action and intentional desire to grow personally and relationally, which takes work. To fuel your intentions, consider a few things. Now that you have the tools, how will you use your tools? What will you do to ensure you maintain the confidence and commitment to take care of your own business and celebrate when you see your husband thriving in his? As you think about your relationship with your husband and all we have learned together, hold on to the beautiful promise that as your husband continues to grow in his gate, you will excel in yours. Your hard work will show.

Celebrate and share in safe places! Letting others know about your triumphs, lessons, and overcoming sharpens your vision with the right perspective and makes deposits of hope into your memory bank.

Who will you share this with?

- your mate
- your marriage mentor
- your little sister who is single
- your women in your network

And that's why I say, *Until we meet again*. It is truly a journey, not a singular sprint to develop all the ability needed to be amazing wives. The ministry of marriage comes with it times of moving full speed ahead and times we feel like we are not moving at all. In those times, I don't want you to feel that you have stalled. I just want you to check under the hood of your relationship and see what needs to be tuned up.

My prayer is that this journey and all the discoveries you documented in this book-turned-personal-business-blueprint can be your resource to get back on the road again. For all the miles ahead, rest stops, and all, let's be in the business of exciting adventures ahead.

_____

_____

_____

_____

Made in the USA
Middletown, DE
21 October 2021

50318221R20070